THE **PRINCETON** REVIEW

CRACKING
THE SAT II:
SPANISH
SUBJECT TEST

13-94

Other books in The Princeton Review Series

Cracking the New SAT and PSAT
Cracking the New SAT and PSAT
Cracking the New SAT and PSAT with Diagnostic Tests on Disk
Cracking the ACT
Cracking the LSAT
Cracking the LSAT with Diagnostic Tests on Disk
Cracking the GRE
Cracking the GRE with Diagnostic Tests on Disk
Cracking the GMAT
Cracking the GMAT with Diagnostic Tests on Disk
Cracking the MCAT
Cracking the SAT II: Biology
Cracking the SAT II: Chemistry
Cracking the SAT II: English
Cracking the SAT II: French
Cracking the SAT II: History
Cracking the SAT II: Math
Cracking the SAT II: Physics
Cracking the TOEFL with audiocassette
How to Survive Without Your Parents' Money
Grammar Smart
Math Smart
Study Smart
Student Access Guide to America's Top 100 Internships
Student Access Guide to College Admissions
Student Access Guide to the Best Business Schools
Student Access Guide to the Best Law Schools
Student Access Guide to the Best Medical Schools
Student Access Guide to Paying for College
Student Access Guide to the Best 286 Colleges
Word Smart: Building a Better Vocabulary
Word Smart II: How to Build a More Educated Vocabulary

Also available on cassette from Living Language

Grammar Smart
Word Smart
Word Smart II

1995 EDITION

THE **PRINCETON** REVIEW

CRACKING THE SAT II: SPANISH SUBJECT TEST

George Roberto Pace

VILLARD BOOKS NEW YORK 1994

Second Edition

• Para Roberto, Carmina, y Enrique, sin quienes no estuviese donde estoy.

• To Ernie and Bert, for helping me learn to speak English.

CONTENTS

THE **PRINCETON** REVIEW

CRACKING THE SAT II:

SPANISH

SUBJECT TEST

CHAPTER ONE

Introduction

Welcome to The Princeton Review

The Princeton Review (TPR) is a company that's been preparing students for standardized tests for the past eleven years. In that short time, we've spread our unique approach to test-taking all over the globe, and more importantly we've changed the way people look at these tests. Our philosophy is simple: standardized tests are biased and unfair, and they reveal nothing about a student other than how well he/she can take a dot test under time pressure. In other words, they're not worth the paper they're printed on. However, until schools stop using these tests as an admission criterion, we will continue to show students how to outsmart them. Students can beat these exams by thoroughly reviewing exactly what is being tested, learning how to avoid trap answers, pacing themselves, and guessing effectively. Our results prove this. We already have courses and books for the PSAT, SAT, GRE, LSAT, GMAT, and MCAT. Now we're taking on the SAT II: Subject Tests.

Why Our Book?

If you take a moment to check out the other prep books on this subject, the first thing you'll notice is that they're outdated: none of them mentions the new four-question format. Our book not only tells you about the new question type that was added, but it also coaches you on how to deal with it and gives examples for you to practice on.

You'll also find that the other books only consist of practice tests. They offer no strategies, no shortcuts, no tips on how to prepare, just practice questions. Practice is definitely important if you want to maximize your score, and this book has plenty of it, with explanations. But if you only do practice questions and never take any time to analyze your performance, rethink your strategy, or review the material that's being tested, those practice questions won't be nearly as useful as they could be. To ace this test, you need to know some Spanish, but you also need to know how to take a test. This is the only book that teaches you both of those things.

What Is the Spanish Subject Test (SST)?

The SAT II: Spanish Subject Test is an hour-long, multiple choice exam which is supposed to measure your knowledge of Spanish. In fact, the College Board (which is just a part of the Educational Testing Service, the same group of bums that writes the Scholastic Aptitude Test) claims that Subject Tests ". . . provide a reliable measure of your academic achievement" and "can help in assessing how well prepared you are for different programs of college study." Does the SAT II: Spanish Subject Test really accomplish this? Absolutely not. If you really want to find out how good your Spanish is, get a Spanish newspaper and see how much of it you can understand, or try to carry on a conversation with a native speaker. Knowing Spanish means being able to communicate in both spoken and written forms, and has nothing to do with being able to do well on a silly test written by gringos. The folks at ETS try to make their test sound like the most important and useful creation since the toothbrush, and it's in their best interests to do so. The fact is that this test, although it might measure a little knowledge of Spanish, mostly measures how well you perform under time restrictions and how well you can take a test.

The test is designed for students who have taken anywhere from two to four years of high school Spanish, and as a result the difficulty of the questions varies a lot. Later on you'll find out how to take advantage of this. For now, let's talk about the test in general.

Why Should You Take It?

The only reason you would possibly have for taking this test is that the colleges you want to get into require (or "highly recommend") that you do. Otherwise, there's no reason to spend the time, energy, or money. The schools that do want you to take subject tests usually request that you take three different ones (Math, English, and Spanish for example), and sometimes even specify which tests they'd prefer you to take. In order to find out about what your target schools want, consult your counselor or give the school a call.

The tests are used in a couple of different ways. Sometimes they're used to place you into the appropriate level freshman courses. In other cases, a good score on an achievement can boost the strength of your application, but for placement purposes the college will give you its own exam when you arrive on campus (usually during orientation week). Yet another possibility is that a school, in spite of requiring subject tests, will actually give them very little weight, if any at all, in deciding your admission status. Why would these schools require that you take three tests and then virtually ignore them? That's a good question, and I have no clue as to what the answer might be.

Structure of the Test

There are four different question types and a total of 85 questions on the test. You're given an hour for the whole test, but the individual sections have no time restrictions. You can do the sections and questions in any order you want.

The structure of the test is as follows:

	QUESTION TYPE	NUMBER OF QUESTIONS
Part A:	Vocabulary and Structure	Approx. 28
Part B:	Paragraph Completion	Approx. 29
Part C:	Reading Comprehension	Approx. 28

Scoring

The SST is scored on a 200–800 scale, with 200 points given to you just for showing up and 800 points representing a perfect score. Your score is determined by taking the number of questions you got right, subtracting 1/3 of the number you got wrong, and multiplying the difference by approximately 7. In other words, every right answer is worth one raw point, and for every wrong answer you lose one-third of a raw point. You are not penalized for questions that you leave blank! Blanks will neither help you nor hurt you.

When Should You Take It?

The SST is given five times a year: in November, December, January, May, and June. There is no better or worse time to take the test, other than whenever you have the most time to prepare. One very important thing to remember is that if you take more than one Subject Test on a certain day, you must either keep or cancel ALL of the tests taken on that day. You can't keep the one you aced and ditch the others. Because of this, it's probably wise to take one or at most two tests at a time and focus your preparation on those instead of trying to study for three at once just to get them over with. To sign up for the SAT, ask your guidance counselor for an application and be sure to send it in early in order to get your first choice of locations.

How to Use This Book

If your goals are to bone up on the material that the SAT tests, learn some test-taking strategies, and apply those strategies on practice questions, then this book contains everything you need. BUT DON'T JUST READ THE BOOK. Spend some time studying both the material and the techniques for each question type. Once you're comfortable with them, do the drill at the end of the chapter, and afterwards review your work to make sure that you applied what you learned in that chapter. The explanations will help guide you through each question. If you find that a certain word or grammatical concept gives you trouble, go back and review that section of the chapter. After you've done this for each question type, take the full-length SST at the back of the book, keeping in mind all of your general strategies as well as those for each question type. When you're done, take a look at your performance in order to adjust your strategy and know what you need to review.

If you want to walk into your SST with as much confidence as possible, and improve your Spanish a bit at the same time, you may want to supplement this book with some reading and conversation. Why? Because speaking and reading the language daily, even for a short time, will expand your vocabulary (which is a big help on this test) and make you more comfortable with Spanish in general.

CHAPTER TWO

How to Take the Test: Overall Strategies

In chapters three through six you'll review the Spanish you need to know (as well as some strategies) for the different question types. Right now, let's talk about how to take a test.

Pacing

Since your earliest days in school, you were probably taught that when you take a test, finishing is important. Your teachers usually gave you plenty of time to finish, and if you couldn't they'd let you return during a free period to let you do the questions you didn't get to answer. In other words, your teachers were interested in how much you knew, not in how fast you could work.

Standardized tests are a completely different ball game. The folks who write these tests are interested in how fast you can work, and in fact they design the tests so that it's nearly impossible to finish on time. However, because you're so accustomed to the idea that finishing is crucial, you may take standardized tests the same way you take all tests: you may pressure yourself to answer every question. Have you ever stopped to consider how much sense this makes? It's not as if you get a special prize for finishing! In fact, in order to finish, you usually have to rush through questions, and as a result you make careless errors that could have been avoided. Doesn't it make more sense to slow down a bit, answer the questions you're sure of, and leave a few blanks? Well, let's see what this would look like on an SAT:

PACING CHART

To Get a	Answer About	Leave This Many Blank
400	13	72
450	26	59
500	38	47
550	48	37
600	58	27
650	68	17
700	78	7
750 & UP	85	0

In general you're going to spend more time on parts A, B, and C, and if there's time left over you might do some of part D. You'll see why when you learn more about the individual question types.

Understand that the pacing chart assumes that you'll make fewer than four mistakes, and it doesn't take guesses into account. If you take your time, pick your questions carefully, and learn to guess effectively, that really isn't as tough as it might sound.

You should walk into your SST with a target score in mind and a pacing strategy that reflects the score you're shooting for. Remember, this is your test, and that means you can answer what questions you want, when you want, how you want, and still get an excellent score. If you want to leave most (or all) of the Reading Comprehension blank and concentrate on the other questions, go ahead. If you're good at the Reading Comp., but not so good on the grammar, then do more of the Reading Comp. and less of the Grammar Sentence Completions. If all the other students at your test site want to race frantically to the end of the test and make careless mistakes along the way, that's their problem. You're going to be sitting there, cool and relaxed, just taking your time and getting a great score.

When Should You Guess?

Each question on the exam has four answer choices, so if you took a completely blind guess you'd have a one-in-four chance of getting that question right. Since you're losing a third of a point if you're wrong, guessing blindly is not in your favor. If, however, you can cancel even one answer choice that you're certain is wrong, then guessing is DEFINITELY a wise thing to do, because the odds are tilted in your favor. If you can cancel one or more answers, guess. When should you skip a question altogether? If all of the vocabulary on a question is too tough, then skip it and look for an easier question. Basically, if you can't cancel anything, or your pacing strategy doesn't allow time to get to a question, leave it blank.

Three-Pass System

Because the test is written for students with varying degrees of experience with Spanish, the questions vary in difficulty. Unfortunately, they aren't arranged in any particular order of difficulty. There are questions that are much easier than others, but it's up to you to find them if you want to take advantage of them.

THE THREE-PASS SYSTEM SAYS THE FOLLOWING:

1st Pass— Go through an entire section of the test from beginning to end, but only answer the easiest questions, that is, those on which you thoroughly understand all the vocabulary, etc. Skip anything that looks as if it's going to give you grief.

2nd Pass— Go back to the beginning of the same section and take a shot at those questions where you knew some, but not all of the vocabulary.

3rd Pass— Use the process of elimination (which you'll learn about in a moment) on the remaining questions in that section, to cancel some answers. Then take a guess. If you can't cancel anything, leave the question blank.

Taking a section of the test this way will keep you from getting stuck on a tough question early in the section and spending too much time on it. Your time should be spent answering questions you're sure of and guessing intelligently, not banging your head against the wall in an attempt to crack a tough question.

POE— Process of Elimination

The usefulness of the process of elimination is one of the gifts of a multiple-choice exam. The idea is simple: knowing which answer is right is the same as knowing which answers are wrong, and so if you can do either you can pick up a point. If you can cancel answers that you know are wrong, you will eventually stumble upon the right answer because it'll be the only one left. You'll learn how this applies to each question type later on. POE is going to vary a bit for the different question types, but the general idea is always the same.

CHAPTER THREE

Vocabulary Sentence Completions

The first section of your SST (part A) will consist of approximately twenty-eight vocabulary and grammar questions. This chapter deals with a question type we call "sentence completion." Each sentence is missing one or more words, and your job is to select the answer choice that best completes the sentence in terms of meaning. In other words, fill in the blank with the answer that makes the most sense. Like all the questions on the test, each of the questions in this section has four answer choices. Before you go any further, memorize the directions to this question type so that you're so familiar with them, you will never have to read them again.

Directions: This part consists of a number of incomplete statements, each having four suggested completions. Select the most appropriate completion and fill in the corresponding oval on the answer sheet.

How to Crack This Section

One of the keys to the Vocabulary Sentence Completions is vocabulary. If you know every word that appears in the section, then understanding the sentences and choosing the right answers is a breeze. So one of the things you're going to work on is improving your vocabulary. Later in this chapter you'll find a list of words that are most likely to appear on your test, along with easy ways to remember them. If you think your vocabulary needs help, then start working on that list TODAY. We'll see more about vocabulary later. What else can be done to attack this question type?

In order to master this section, you need to combine your vocabulary review with some common sense. You've already read about pacing, POE, and the three-pass system in general. Now you're going to learn how those ideas apply to this section in particular, as well as learn some additional techniques that are designed just for this question type.

First Pass:
When You Understand the Entire Sentence

It's pretty obvious that the easiest questions for you to deal with are those on which you understand the entire sentence. You should do these questions first. Remember, the questions are not in any particular order of difficulty, so it's up to you to hunt down the easiest ones. Your approach should be to read the sentence, and if it's easy, then to answer that question. If you're a bit uncomfortable with some of the vocabulary, move on and come back to that question later during your second pass.

Be careful. Just because a question is a "first-pass question" doesn't mean you should blow through it as fast as possible and risk making a careless error. Once you've decided to answer a question on the first pass, take the following steps:

THINK OF YOUR OWN WORD

The first step after reading the sentence is to fill in the blank with your own word without peeking at the answers. Your word doesn't have to be long or difficult, and in fact short and simple is best. Also, your word doesn't even have to be in Spanish. If it's easier for you to think in English, then write the word in English. The important thing is to choose a word that fits in terms of meaning. After you have a word, write it down next to your sentence (or in the actual blank, if there's room). Try this on the following example:

> Hoy hace mucho frío. Por eso voy a ponerme un ...

What would make sense in this blank? Well, pretty much anything that had to do with cold (frío), like a pair of gloves (par de guantes) or a sweater (suéter). You shouldn't feel that there's only one possible answer, because there are usually several words that would make sense in the blank. Don't worry about picking the <u>right</u> word, just worry about picking a word that makes sense. Once you've done this, move on to the next step.

CANCEL ANSWERS THAT ARE OUT OF THE BALLPARK

Now you're going to look at the answers and cross out any answer that does not fall into the same category as your word. You're not looking for the right answer, you're looking to cancel wrong answers.

Let's say that you filled in the word "suéter" in the example above. Which of the following answer choices would you cancel?

A) vestido
B) abrigo
C) zapato
D) lápiz

Does a dress (vestido), shoe (zapato), or pencil (lápiz) have anything at all to do with cold or a sweater? No, and so the correct choice is B. If you don't know all of the words in the answers, then cancel whichever ones you can and take a guess at the remaining choices.

AVOID TRAP ANSWERS

Once you've filled in your own word, it's crucial that you don't just pick the first answer you see that reminds you of the word you came up with. The folks who write this test are very clever about creating answer choices that are tempting but incorrect. Knowing what types of traps they typically lay out for you will help you to avoid them. In this section, there are a couple of tricks that show up frequently:

ANSWERS THAT SOUND ALIKE:

One way the test writers try to confuse you is by having all four answers sound alike, even though their meanings are different. You can easily avoid these by reading carefully and not using your ear. Remember that you're picking the best answer based on meaning, not on how it sounds. Try the following example:

> La madre de Pedro no le dejó salir porque todavía no había ... su cuarto.
>
> A) llamado
> B) limpiado
> C) llevado
> D) llenado

Why wouldn't a mom allow her son to go out? Probably because he hadn't cleaned his room. The word for clean is **limpiar** and, since we're in the past perfect, **limpiado** would be the correct form (if that doesn't make sense, don't fret—the grammar review is in the next chapter, and you don't need to be the Mad Grammarian to do well on this test). Notice how all the other answers sound very similar to **limpiado**. This is why it's important to take your time and to concentrate on meaning.

CATEGORIES:

Another favorite trick of the test writers is to give you four things that all come from the same category, as in the following example:

> Ricardo quiere lavarse las manos, y por eso necesita ...
>
> A) un cepillo
> B) una navaja
> C) pasta de dientes
> D) jabón

Each of the answer choices is something you'd find in a bathroom (**jabón** = soap, **navaja** = razor, **pasta de dientes** = toothpaste, **cepillo** = hairbrush). Although these words have very different meanings, seeing them all together like this may be confusing, especially if you're thinking in general terms (bathroom stuff) and not in terms of the specific word you chose for the blank. For this reason it's very important that you fill the blank with a specific word, and not a general category.

Second Pass:
When You <u>Don't</u> Understand the Entire Sentence

Let's say you've answered all of the questions where you found the sentence to be easy. Now what? The strategy for first-pass questions works just fine when you have a clear understanding of the sentence, but unfortunately there will probably be some words that you don't know in some of the sentences. Will that keep you from answering the question altogether? Absolutely not, but you will leave these questions for the second pass. The approach is different for these questions, but it works just as well as the approach for the first-pass questions. Not knowing some of the vocabulary will hardly be a handicap at all if you are aggressive and use POE, so don't let these questions intimidate you!

SESAME STREET TECHNIQUE, A.K.A. ONE OF THESE THINGS IS NOT LIKE THE OTHERS

One of the nice things about this question type (from your point of view) is that the answer choices are usually very far apart in meaning. In other words, you <u>rarely</u> find two answers that are separated by subtle shades of meaning. Instead you find four things that have nothing to do with each other, except perhaps a very general common category, similar to what you saw earlier in the "avoid trap answers" section. Why is this so helpful? It allows you to cancel answer choices based on a minimal understanding of the sentence. If you can figure out the general context of the sentence by piecing together one or two words as clues, you can eliminate answers that are unlikely to appear in that context. You'll usually find that there's really only one word that makes any kind of sense in that context. Choose the answer that is <u>not</u> like the others.

> Eduardo se monta en el automóvil y dice ...
>
> A) tengo hambre
> B) hace mucho calor
> C) el perro es grande
> D) necesito gasolina

What if the only word you understand in the above sentence is "automóvil"? Well, your next thought should be, "Which of the answers has a word that has something to do with a car?" Answer A, which means "I'm hungry," doesn't seem likely. Answer B talks about the weather, which isn't a car-related topic. Choice C probably wins the prize for most ridiculous: "the dog is big." So which answer is not like the others? Choice D, which means "I need gas." Notice that not only do you not need to understand the entire sentence, but also you don't even need to understand the entire set of answer choices. If you can make out some of the key words in either the sentence or the answers, you can eliminate some of the answer choices.

It's important to understand that this technique will <u>not</u> always leave you with only one remaining answer, i.e., the right one. Sometimes you will be able to eliminate one or two choices and end up taking an educated guess. However, guessing one out of two is much better than guessing one out of four. Never cancel an answer simply because you don't understand it. If you're not sure, leave it in and deal with the choices that you are sure of. Also, the technique allows you to get around some of the tough vocabulary, but you still need to know the meanings of some of the words in order to use the technique: if you don't know what the answers mean, you can't determine which one is not like the others. The moral of the story is DON'T NEGLECT YOUR VOCABULARY WORK!!

DRILL:

In the following drill, each sentence is missing all but a couple of key words. Eliminate answers that aren't related to the words in the sentence. If you're left with more than one answer, guess the one that is most like the words in the sentence.

1) Maria *blah blah blah* médico *blah blah* ...

    (A) enferma
    (B) perfumada
    (C) acostada
    (D) sucia

2) *Blah blah blah* revistas *blah blah blah* ...

    (A) vacaciones
    (B) obras de teatro
    (C) conciertos
    (D) artículos interesantes

3) No *blah* salír porque *blah* mucha ...

    (A) comida
    (B) dinero
    (C) nieve
    (D) hambre

4) *Blah* postre me *blah blah* que ...

   (A) el agua
   (B) las vitaminas
   (C) el helado
   (D) arroz con pollo

5) La película *blah blah blah* miedo porque *blah blah* ...

   (A) violenta
   (B) graciosa
   (C) corta
   (D) tremenda

6) La casa *blah blah* sucia. *Blah blah* que ...

   (A) llorar
   (B) limpiar
   (C) llover
   (D) llevar

Answers: 1) A 2) D 3) C 4) C 5) A 6) B

EXPLANATIONS:

1) A **Médico** (doctor) would make **enferma** (ill) a very good guess. The other answers (**perfumada** = scented, **acostada** = lying down, **sucia** = dirty) have nothing to do with doctor.

2) D **Revistas** (magazines) would match up with **artículos interesantes** (interesting articles) better than it would with any of the other choices offered (**vacaciones** = vacations, **obras de teatro** = plays, **conciertos** = concerts)

3) C This is a pretty tough one, but you can still take a good guess. **Salir** (go out), combined with the **no** that precedes it gives you "no go out." Are any of the answers something that might keep you from going out? Yes, **nieve** (snow). None of the others would really make sense (**comida** = food, **dinero** = money, **hambre** = hunger).

4) C **Postre** means dessert, and there is only one answer that is a dessert: **helado** (ice cream). **Arroz con pollo** (chicken with rice), **vitaminas** (vitamins), and **agua** (water) are all edible, but they aren't desserts.

5) A If you put **película** (movie) and **miedo** (fear) together, what do you get? A scary movie! The closest guess would be **violenta** (violent). **Graciosa** means funny, **corta** means short, and **tremenda** means huge or grand.

6) B **Sucia** (which, as you saw earlier, means dirty) is enough to tell you to guess **limpia** (clean). **Casa** (house) doesn't really give you any additional helpful information. **Llorar** (to cry), **llover** (to rain), and **llevar** (to take) all sound similar to the right answer, but their meanings are way off.

Third Pass:
When You Hardly Understand Any Part of the Sentence

These questions should be left for last: there's very little you can do if you know only one or two words in the entire sentence. Your goal on the third pass is to go back to those questions that you skipped on the first two passes and see if you can eliminate even one answer choice based on the word or words that you do know in the sentence, using the same approach that you used on the second pass. The only difference is you'll probably have less to base your decision on. If you're unable to cancel anything, no sweat—just move on to the next question.

You don't need to know the hardest words in the sentence in order to knock off some of the answers. Even if you can only determine that the answer is going to be a feminine word based on its article (**la**), that alone could get rid of one or two choices, so be aggressive!

SUMMARY

FIRST PASS: WHEN YOU UNDERSTAND THE ENTIRE SENTENCE
- fill in your own word (short and simple)
- cancel answers that are not in the same category as your word
- beware of their little traps: concentrate on meaning, not sound
- pick the one that's closest to your word out of the remaining choices

SECOND PASS: WHEN YOU DON'T UNDERSTAND THE ENTIRE SENTENCE
- determine the meanings of as many individual words as you can
- put these words together to try and determine the general context of the sentence
- cancel any choices that don't make sense in that context
- pick the one that is most likely to appear in the context out of the remaining choices (it should be the only one left)

THIRD PASS: WHEN YOU HARDLY UNDERSTAND ANY PART OF THE SENTENCE
- try to locate sentences where you know at least one or two words
- see if any of the answers seem impossible based on those words
- cancel those answers and guess

NEVER . . .
- cancel an answer choice because you don't know its meaning—just because you don't know it doesn't mean it's wrong! Use POE on the words you *do* know
- leave a question blank if you can eliminate even one answer—the odds are with you if you can cancel one or more of the choices, so guess!

Practice Questions
Part A

<u>Directions</u>: This part consists of a number of incomplete statements, each having four suggested completions. Select the most appropriate completion and blacken the corresponding space on the answer sheet.

1. El ... que se pone mi novia huele como las rosas.

   (A) calcetín
   (B) esfuerzo
   (C) perfume
   (D) tamaño

2. Buscaba las medicinas para mi abuelo en la ... de la esquina.

   (A) librería
   (B) farmacia
   (C) oficina
   (D) panadería

3. Estaba ... cuando mis empleados llegaron tarde por la cuarta vez en la misma semana.

   (A) furioso
   (B) encantado
   (C) contentísimo
   (D) abierto

4. Si no comes el ... por la mañana no tendrás energía durante el día.

   (A) café
   (B) almuerzo
   (C) caballo
   (D) desayuno

5. Es un hombre sumamente vanidoso; siempre se está mirando en el ...

   (A) espejo
   (B) cristal
   (C) gafas
   (D) mismo

6. Los viejos tienen más ... que los jovenes porque
   han tenido mas experiencias.

   (A) tiempo
   (B) de comer
   (C) sabiduría
   (D) apetito

7. Es bastante evidente que a Alejandro le gusta
   hacer la tarea; siempre la hace ...

   (A) de mala gana
   (B) con entusiasmo
   (C) muy despacio
   (D) sin gusto

8. Pedro ... muy contento cuando nació su hijo.

   (A) se cambió
   (B) se dio
   (C) se hizo
   (D) se puso

Answers and Explanations to Practice Questions: Part A

1. The ... that my girlfriend puts on smells like roses.

   A) sock
   B) effort
   C) perfume
   D) size

The key word in this sentence is **huele**, which is an excellent clue because the only answer that is related to smell is **perfume**.

2. I was looking for my grandfather's medicines in the ... on the corner.

   A) book store
   B) pharmacy
   C) office
   D) bakery

The clue in this question is a cognate (remember those?), **medicinas**, so that even if the rest of the sentence was a blur you could tell that the answer had something to do with medicines. The answer also happens to be a cognate, and is the only choice that relates to medicines.

3. I was ... when my employees arrived late for the fourth time in the same week.

   A) furious
   B) delighted
   C) very happy
   D) open

Unless you were some sort of lunatic, you'd be pretty peeved if your staff was late all the time. Although three of the answers are emotions, only one of the three is a negative emotion.

4. If you don't eat ... in the morning you won't have
energy during the day.

    A) coffee
    B) lunch
    C) horse
    D) breakfast

Comes and **por la mañana** are the two key words here. What do you eat in the morning? Breakfast, of course. **Café** isn't a bad second choice, but the problem with it is that you drink it, you don't eat it and the verb that comes before the blank is **comer**. Even though the meaning comes across, you should never use **comer** with **café**.

5. He is an extremely vain man: he's always looking
at himself in the ...

    A) mirror
    B) glass
    C) glasses
    D) self

Vano is one clue in this one, but that's a pretty tough vocabulary word (add it to your list). You've also got **mirarse** (to look at oneself) later in the sentence to tell you that the best answer is **espejo**. **Cristal** means plain old glass, like in a window or a bottle.

6. Old people have more ... than young people because they've had more experiences.

    A) time
    B) to eat
    C) wisdom
    D) appetite

Old folks probably have more of lots of things than do young folks, but what might they have more of based on experience? Not time, food, or appetite, which leaves you with only C. We know this is a hard word, but you could have used POE to get this question right without knowing **sabiduría**.

7. It's pretty obvious that Alejandro likes doing his
    homework; he always does it ...

    (A) begrudgingly
    (B) eagerly
    (C) very slowly
    (D) without taste

"Likes" implies a positive answer, such as B. The others are all negative things, and if you could determine that much you could cancel them without knowing their precise meanings.

8. Pedro ... very happy when his child was born.

    (A) changed
    (B) gave himself
    (C) made himself
    (D) became

Choices A and B are really awkward, and although C could work, D is a better answer. A person could make him or herself happy, but that suggests a conscious effort, which is probably unnecessary in this context.

Vocabulary Review

WHY WORK ON YOUR VOCABULARY?

In case you haven't already noticed, vocabulary is a very important part of this test. You've already seen some ways to get around the tough vocabulary by using certain techniques, but that doesn't mean that you can blow off this section of the book. We know, we know—memorizing vocabulary words is about as much fun as watching grass grow. At the same time, vocabulary work can translate into some easy points on the day of the test: if you know the words, the questions are that much easier. By not working on your vocabulary, you're blowing a golden opportunity to improve your score. We've narrowed down your work so that you're only dealing with the words that are most likely to appear on the test. Now it's up to you to memorize them.

HOW TO USE THIS LIST

The following list of words is broken down by category, and you should memorize it that way. Why? First of all, it's easier to memorize words in organized groups than in one big list. Second, the test writers will try to trip you up by giving you answer choices from the same category (see "Categories" on page 16), so you are more likely to avoid this trap if you memorize the words by category.

Your first step is to go through the list and check off the words that you are familiar and comfortable with (there's no need to bore yourself to death by relearning what you already know). Afterward, simply go in order and start memorizing the words by category. The first batch ("Don't forget to use your English") should take less time, because the Spanish words are so close to their English equivalents that you'll probably remember their meanings even if you don't spend loads of time reviewing them. Spend more of your time on the words that aren't similar in English and Spanish. Make flash cards. Have your family members drill you. Put up lists of words that are particularly difficult in your shower. Do whatever you have to do, just memorize these words!

NOTE: One special category that follows contains words that are grouped by their similarity to English, not by subject. These are called cognates (words that are virtually the same in two different languages, both in meaning and in appearance). Be careful: there are also <u>false</u> cognates (words that look alike, but don't have the same meaning), so don't assume that similar-looking words necesssarily mean the same thing. It could just be a nasty trap. For example, the Spanish word **playa** does NOT mean "play," it means "beach."

Don't forget to use your English . . .
Words and expressions that are very similar in English and Spanish:

SPANISH WORD EQUIVALENT	ENGLISH
profundo	profound; deep
participar	participate
el automóvil	automobile
el circo	circus
un minuto	minute
la sopa	soup
el perfume	perfume
el periódico	newspaper (periodical)
el disgusto	disgust
el/la dentista	dentist
las encías	gums
la farmacia	pharmacy
el libro	book (think "library")
la música	music
estupendo/a	stupendous
el médico	doctor (think "medicine")
la librería	library
el crítico	critic
criticar	to criticize
la ovación	ovation
el plato	plate
preocupado/a	preoccupied
el programa de televisión	television program
el apetito	appetite
la vacación	vacation
el teatro	theater
la biología	biology
el empleado, la empleada	employee
el arte	art
el/la artista	artist
la controversia	controversy
la creación	creation
el hotel	hotel
la manifestación	manifestation
furioso/a	furious
cordial	cordial, polite

la residencia	residence, home
practicar	practice
la operación	operation
el estómago	stomach
falso	false, fake
decidir	to decide
participar	to participate
el caso	case (as in "in this case," not suitcase)
el dependiente	dependent
la clase	class (as in school, or society)
defender	to defend, protect
la gloria	glory
misterioso/a	mysterious
impresión	impression
plantar	to plant
servir	to serve
contemporáneo/a	contemporary
el campo	countryside, field
el verso	verse
el acta	act (as in a play)
la criatura	creature; infant, baby
la gracia	grace, attractiveness

BASIC WORDS AND PHRASES YOU SHOULD KNOW: ASSORTED TOPICS

por eso	that's why . . .
la noticia	news
cada uno	each one
poner	to put
sentado/a	seated
dormido/a	asleep
llamar	to call
muy poco	very little
manejar	to drive
entrar	to enter
¿quién eres?	who are you?
llevar	to take, to carry
tocar	to touch
tocar a la puerta	to knock at the door
el correo	mail

el buzón de correo	mailbox
sacar	to take out, to remove
la vuelta	turn (as in "my turn")
dar la vuelta	to turn or flip over
la carrera	race
el negocio	business
sin falta	without fail
terminar	to finish
la calidad	quality
la cantidad	quantity
la revista	magazine
mostrar	to show
el partido	party (as in political, not birthday); game, match
el árbol	tree
devolver	to give back
el almacén	warehouse
el desfile	parade, procession
advertir	to notice, observe; to warn
el estilo	style
tener cuidado	to be careful
envolver	to wrap
ahorrar	to save (as in money, not a life)
algo	something
empezar	to begin

WE ARE FAMILY . . .

la madre	mother
el padre	father (also sometimes used for priest)
hijo/hija	son/daughter
tío/tía	uncle/aunt
sobrino/sobrina	nephew/niece
primo/prima	cousin (m/f)
nieto/nieta	grandson/grandaughter
niño/niña	boy/girl (usually used for small children)
muchacho/muchacha	boy/girl (usually used for teenagers)
abuelo/abuela	grandfather/grandmother
hermano/hermana	brother/sister

SCHOOL DAYS . . .

despiértate	wake up!
levántate	get up!
la escuela	school
a tiempo	on time
tarde	late
la tarde	afternoon
el trabajo	work
la tarea	homework
hacer la tarea	to do homework
leer	to read
el cuento	story
saber	to know
escribir	to write
la librería	bookstore
el libro	book
el número	number
tonto/a	bone-headed, dense
estudiar	to study
los estudiantes	students
prestar atención	to pay attention
el idioma	language
preguntar	to ask

FEED ME!

apetito	appetite
tener hambre	to be hungry
comer	to eat
beber	to drink
la comida	food
camarero/a	waiter/waitress
la cuenta	the check, the bill
el desayuno	breakfast
el arroz	rice
el pollo	chicken
gordo/a	fat
delgado/a	thin
el vaso	glass
la taza	cup
el helado	ice cream
el olor	smell, odor, aroma
el sabor	flavor

THE NECK BONE'S CONNECTED TO THE . . .

los dientes	teeth
las encías	gums
la muela	molar
el estómago	stomach
las manos	hands
la cintura	waist
la cabeza	head

SHOPPING IS MY LIFE . . .

comprar	to buy
ir de compras	to go shopping
la camiseta	T-shirt
la cartera	purse, wallet
la zapatería	shoe store
la corbata	tie
el pañuelo	handkerchief
el calcetín	sock (also used to mean condom)
el vestido	dress
el abrigo	coat
el dinero	money
los dólares	dollars
de lujo	expensive, luxurious
gastar dinero	spend money

AN APPLE A DAY . . .

la úlcera	ulcer
diagnosticar	to diagnose
la operación	operation
la extracción	extraction
pálido/a	pale
la herida	injury, wound
enfermo/a	sick
sufrir	to suffer
el dolor	pain
el médico	doctor
el/la dentista	dentist
la salud	health

HOUSE STUFF . . .

la casa	house
el piso	floor
el suelo	floor (usually outdoors, as in ground)
las muebles	furniture
la butaca	armchair, easy chair
salir	to go out
volver	to return
el espejo	mirror
el jabón	soap
el sillón	rocking chair; armchair
lavar	to wash
limpiar	to clean

COMPARATIVELY SPEAKING . . .

antes	before
después	after
demasiado/a	too (as in too much, too late, too funny, etc.)
mayor	older
menor	younger
mejor	better
peor	worse
mediocre	mediocre
bien hecho	well done

THE MEANING OF LIFE . . .

la vida	life
cambiar	to change
con cariño	with affection
los chistes	jokes
reír	to laugh
regalar	to give as a gift
ganar	to win
saber	to know
sabiduría	knowledge, wisdom
jugar	to play
aceptar	to accept
ofrecer	to offer
querer	to want; to love (te quiero = I love you)

llegar a viejo	to reach old age
tranquilo/a	peaceful, tranquil
reposar	to rest, relax
desear	to want
esperar	to wait
odiar	to loathe, hate
decir	to say
es decir	that is, . . .
tener	to have
buscar	to look for, search for
hacer	to do
sentir	to feel
¿como te sientes?	how do you feel?
simpatía	sympathy
la pena	sorrow, trouble
escoger	to choose
prestar	to lend
empeñarse	to pledge or devote oneself

TOO MUCH TIME ON MY HANDS . . .

la última vez	last time
el siglo	century
el centenario	centennial
despacio	slow, slowly
en cuanto	as soon as
inmediatamente	immediately
durante	during
empezar	to begin
acabar	to finish
hace un rato	a little while ago . . .
próximo/a	next
el próximo día	the next day
media hora	half hour
la hora	hour, time
¿Qué hora es?	What time is it?
de la noche	P.M.
de la mañana	A.M.
apurarse	to hurry oneself
en marcha	on the move, on the go
ahora mismo	right now
la fecha	date (as in calendar)
¿A cómo estamos?	What's the date?

hoy	today
mañana	tomorrow
la mañana	morning
ayer	yesterday
cada vez	each time
el año	year
en seguida	right away
de buena gana	when I feel like it, when I get around to it
alrededor de	around (alrededor de las ocho = around 8:00)

PLACES TO GO, PEOPLE TO SEE . . .

ir	to go
la esquina	corner, street corner
la playa	the beach
la obra de teatro	the play
la taquilla	box office
cerca de	near
la calle	street
el viaje	trip
aquí	here
allí	there
el mapa	map
dondequiera	wherever
la ciudad	city
el país	country
la película	movie
el recital	recital
el banco	bank
el camino	path, route
el señor	gentleman
el hombre	man
el torero	bullfighter
el cartero	postman

HOW'S THE WEATHER?

hacer frío	to be cold out
hacer calor	to be hot out
caliente	hot
caluroso/a	warm, hot
llover/la lluvia	to rain/rain

mojado/mojada	wet
oscuro/a	dark
nevar/la nieve	to snow/snow
el sol	the sun

MUSIC SOOTHES THE SAVAGE BEAST . . .

la música	music
la orquesta	orchestra
tocar	to play (as in an instrument); to touch
practicar	to practice

LIFE'S A DRAG . . .

nada más	no more, nothing more
¡de ninguna forma!	no way!
nadie	no one
¡ya lo creo!	yeah, right! (sarcastic)
ningún / ninguna	(adj.) no
con disgusto	with disgust
falsamente	falsely
regañar	to punish
romper	to break
tener culpa	to be at fault, guilty
sin querer	unintentionally; against your will
el mendigo	beggar
pedir limosna	to beg
con qué derecho . . .	how dare you . . .
quemar	to burn
rechazar	to push away, repel, reject
olvidar	to forget
sucio/a	dirty
quejarse	to complain
grave	serious
distraído	absent-minded
ponerle fin a	to put an end to
de mala gana	reluctantly, begrudgingly
de mal humor	in a bad mood
a contrapelo	the wrong way
inconveniente	unsuitable, inappropriate; inconvenient

LIFE'S A BOWL OF CHERRIES!

perfumada	scented, sweet smelling
cómodo/a	comfortable
lleno/a	full
por favor	please
el premio	prize
premio gordo	grand prize
cómo que no!	of course; I'd be glad to
empeñarse	to pledge or vow
felicitaciones!	congratulations!
cortés	courteous
cordial	cordial
estar de acuerdo	to be in agreement
que Díos lo ampare	may God bless you
el regalo	gift
regalo de cumpleaños	birthday gift
bastante	enough
gracioso/a	cute, funny

REFLEXIVE VERBS

ponerse	to put on oneself; to become
hacerse	to make oneself
acostarse	to lie oneself down
envolverse	to involve oneself with

PREPOSITIONAL PHRASES

a fondo	thoroughly
por regla general	in general, generally
falta de	lack of
en vez de	instead of
acabar de . . .	to have just . . .
fuera de	outside of
vestido de	dressed as
dirigirse a	to address (as in speak to)
dejar de	to cease
a pesar de	despite; in spite of
a mediados de	halfway through

CHAPTER FOUR

Grammar Sentence Completions

O.K., so we're done with the vocabulary sentence completion part of Part A. The rest of Part A focuses on grammar rather than vocabulary. The good news is that you don't need to review everything about grammar that you ever learned, because only a small portion of Spanish grammar is actually tested, and your review will focus on that portion. The even better news is that the techniques you learned earlier work really well on this section, and by combining them with a brief review of some grammar you can do very nicely. Before you get into strategies or review, memorize the instructions to the question type:

> Directions: This part consists of a number of incomplete statements, each having four suggested completions. Select the most appropriate completion and fill in the corresponding oval on the answer sheet.

Each question will be followed by four answer choices. These differ from the vocabulary sentence completion questions because the answer choices will all have the same or very similar meanings, but only one of them will fit the blank and make the sentence grammatically correct. It's not about vocabulary; it's about verbs, pronouns, prepositions, and idioms, but don't let that scare you! After you get through this chapter you'll know everything you need to know.

How to Crack This Section

As much as we hate to admit it, this section does test some knowledge of grammar. The key is to focus specifically on those grammatical concepts that are being tested and spend a little time relearning them. Contrary to what the test writers would like you to believe, this test doesn't nearly test everything you learned in Spanish class, but instead it sticks to a few grammatical ideas and tests them over and over again. You probably already know and are comfortable with many of them, and even if you're not right now, you will be if you invest a little time in studying.

In addition to reviewing the grammar, you will use Process of Elimination and the three-pass system to beat this section. You'll supplement both of these with what may be your best friend on these questions: your ear. Remember how your ear could easily steer you wrong on vocabulary sentence completions because of the way the wrong answers sometimes sounded like the right one? Well, on this section your ear, or how the answers sound, can actually help you eliminate answers right off the bat without using grammar at all. This won't work on all questions, but it certainly will on some, and you're going to take full advantage of this.

FIRST PASS: I'M SURE I'VE SEEN THIS SOMEWHERE BEFORE

Again, the questions are is not arranged in any particular order of difficulty, but the level of difficulty of the different questions varies tremendously. Your goal on the first pass is to locate the questions that test the verb tenses, pronouns, prepositions, and idioms that you know like the back of your hand. Find the easiest questions, and do them first. How do you tell whether a question is easy? Read it, and if the structure looks familiar, go for it. If it looks as if it's going to take a little POE to crack it, leave that question for the second pass.

SECOND PASS: HAVEN'T I SEEN THIS SOMEWHERE BEFORE?

If you read a question and the answer doesn't immediately jump off the page at you, don't be discouraged: just because you don't immediately know what the answer <u>is</u> doesn't mean you can't tell what the answer <u>isn't</u>. Work backwards from the answer choices and eliminate answers that you know are wrong. If you understand some of the answer choices and know that they're wrong, it's just as effective as knowing which one is right. Take a look at the following example:

> Si _____ en el banco, pudiéramos conseguir dinero.
>
> (A) estamos
> (B) estemos
> (C) estuviéramos
> (D) estuvimos

You might read this and think "what tense is that?!"; but let's take a look at what the answers have to offer. All of the answers are some form of the verb **estar**, and although that's one of the trickier verbs, you probably know the tenses in A and B, and maybe even D. Even if you don't know what tense the sentence is in, you can definitely count out the plain old present (cancel choice A) and the present subjunctive (cancel choice B). Choice D is the preterite, which is sort of a past-ish tense, and since this sentence doesn't contain anything that tells you we're in the past, C is a pretty good guess (and in fact it's correct).

THIRD PASS: I'VE NEVER SEEN THIS ANYWHERE

If the grammar in the sentence and the answers is completely foreign to you, chances are you won't be able to back into the right answer using POE. Eliminate anything you can and guess. The most important thing about the third pass (on any section) is that you don't spend too much time on these really tough questions.

Grammar Review

Although we certainly can't lie to you by saying that reviewing grammar rules <u>will</u> be fun, we can promise you that a little time on this material will mean easy points for you on the day of the test. Grammar is merely a bunch of rules, and once you've learned the ones that are tested you'll be ready for this question type.

BASIC TERMS

The following terms, although you won't see them on the test, are important because they will come up later in the chapter. Knowing them will allow you to understand better the rules of grammar that you're about to review.

Noun:	a person, place, or thing. EXAMPLES: Abraham Lincoln, New Jersey, a taco
Pronoun:	a word that replaces a noun. EXAMPLES: Abe Lincoln would be replaced by "he," New Jersey by "it," and a taco by "it." You'll see more about pronouns later.
Adjective:	a word that describes a noun. EXAMPLES: cold, soft, colorful
Verb:	an action word. It is what is being done in a sentence. EXAMPLE: Ron *ate* the huge breakfast
Infinitive:	the original/unconjugated form of a verb. EXAMPLES: to eat, to run, to laugh
Auxiliary Verb:	the verb that precedes the past participle in the past tense. EXAMPLE: He *has* practiced a lot lately.
Past Participle:	the appropriate form of a verb when it is used in the past tense. EXAMPLE: The toy was *broken*.

Adverb: an adverb describes a verb, just like an adjective describes a noun.
EXAMPLES: slowly, quickly, happily
(Adverbs often, but don't always, end in -ly.)

Subject: the thing (noun) in a sentence that is performing the action.
EXAMPLE: *John* wrote the song.

Compound: a subject that's made up of two or more subjects or nouns.
EXAMPLE: *John and Paul* wrote the song together.

Object: the thing (noun or pronoun) in the sentence that the action is happening to.
EXAMPLES: Mary gave the gift to *Tim*. Mary bought *the shirt*. Joe hit *him*.

Direct Object: an object that doesn't take a preposition.
(see the 2nd example under "Object")

Indirect Object: an object that does take a preposition.
(see the 1st example under "Object")

Preposition: a word that marks the relationship between two other words.
EXAMPLES: She gave the letter *to* the postman. He received the letter *from* her.

Article: a word (usually a very small word) that precedes a noun.
EXAMPLES: *a* watch, *the* room

That wasn't so bad, was it? Now let's put all those terms together in a couple of examples:

Dominic spent the entire night trying to finish his play.

subject   past part. article adjective noun   verb   infinitive   object

Margaret   often   gives   money   to   charity.
subject   adverb   verb   dir.obj.   prep.   indir.obj.

Alison   and   Rob   have   a   gorgeous   home.
comp.subj.   verb   article   adj.   obj.

Once you've spent a little time with these terms, go on to the review of the grammar that you'll actually be tested on.

Pronouns

You already learned that a pronoun is a word that takes the place of a noun. Now you'll review what pronouns look like in Spanish, and learn how they are tested on the SAT.

WHAT YOU NEED TO KNOW
If you can tell the difference between subject, object, direct object, and indirect object pronouns, you are in very good shape. Beyond those different types, there are a couple of odds and ends that may show up, but the majority of questions that test pronouns will focus on these four basic types.

SUBJECT PRONOUNS
These are the most basic pronouns, and probably the first ones you learned. Just take a moment to look them over to make sure you haven't forgotten them. Then spend some time looking over the examples that follow until you are comfortable with using them.

yo	I	**nosotros/nosotras**	we
tú	you	**ustedes**	you (plural)
ella/él	she/he	**ellas/ellos**	they

When to Use Subject Pronouns
A subject pronoun (like any other pronoun) replaces a noun, but more specifically it replaces the noun that is the subject of the sentence.

Marco no pudo comprar el helado.
Marco couldn't buy the ice cream.

Who's the subject in this sentence? Marco, so if we wanted to use a subject pronoun in this case, we'd replace "Marco" with "él":

Él no pudo comprar el helado.
He couldn't buy the ice cream.

DIRECT OBJECT PRONOUNS

Direct object pronouns replace (you guessed it) the direct object in a sentence.

me	me	**nos**	us
te	you	**los**	them (mas.)
lo/la	him, it (mas.)/her, it (fem.)	**las**	them (fem.)

When to Use Direct Object Pronouns

Now let's see what it looks like when we replace the dirct object in a sentence with a pronoun:

Marco no pudo comprar el helado.

What's the direct object in this sentence? The ice cream is what's receiving the action, so that's the direct object. To use the direct object pronoun, you'd replace **helado** with **lo**:

Marco no pudo comprar**lo**.

In general, an object pronoun comes before the verb, but in the case of an affirmative command (cómelo!) or when it follows an infinitive (comprarlo) it comes after the verb.

When the direct object pronoun is used with the infinitive of a verb, it can either be tacked on to the end of the verb, or it can come before the first verb in the sentence:

Voy a ver**lo**.   Both mean the same thing
Lo voy a ver.   (I'm going to see it.).

INDIRECT OBJECT PRONOUNS

These pronouns replace the indirect object in a sentence. The indirect object is easy to spot in English because a preposition often comes before it. However, **this is not the case in Spanish**. In Spanish, when

\

the object is indirect, the preposition is implied, not explicitly stated. (There are some pronouns that do take prepositions in Spanish, but they're coming up later in a separate category— it's easier to remember them that way.) So how can you tell the difference? Think in terms of English to determine whether the pronoun is direct or indirect, then translate into Spanish.

me	(to/for) me		**nos**	(to/for) us
te	(to/for) you		**les**	(to/for) them, you
le	(to/for) him, her, it, or you			

When to Use Indirect Object Pronouns

This might seem a bit strange, but in Spanish the indirect object pronoun is usually present in a sentence that contains the indirect object noun:

> Juan le da el abrigo al viejo.
> Juan gives the coat to the old man.

Notice that the sentence contains the indirect object noun (al viejo) and the indirect object pronoun (le). If you want to use only the indirect object pronoun, simply omit the noun:

> Juan le da el abrigo.
> Juan gives him the coat.

"Se" is used in place of "le" and "les" whenever the pronoun that follows begins with "l":

> Le cuentas la notícia **a Maria**?
> Si, **se** la cuento.

> Le prestas los guantes **a los estudiantes**?
> No, no **se** los presto.

(Otherwise you would have to say "le la cuento" and "les los presto," which sound very silly. Perhaps that's why they change "le" and "les" to "se.")

PREPOSITIONAL PRONOUNS

As we mentioned earlier, there are some pronouns that take an explicitly stated preposition, and they're different from the indirect object pronouns. The prepositional pronouns are as follows:

mí	me	**nosotros/as**	us
ti	you	**ustedes**	you (plural)
él/ella	him/her	**ellos/ellas**	them
usted	you		

When to Use Prepositional Pronouns

Consider the following examples:

1) Cómprale un regalo de cumpleaños.   Buy (for) him a birthday present.

2) Vamos al teatro **sin** él.   We're going to the theater **without** him.

Notice that in the first example "him" is translated as "le," whereas in the second "him" is translated as "el." What exactly is the deal with that?! Why isn't it the same word in Spanish as it is in English? Well, we don't really know why, but we can tell you how to distinguish them.

It's actually kind of simple if you remember this basic difference: If the preposition is implied (like the "for" in example 1), then use the indirect object pronoun (like in example 1). If the preposition is explicitly stated (like the "without" in example 2), use the prepositional pronoun. Here are some more examples that involve the prepositional pronouns. Notice that they all have the explicitly stated preposition.

Las flores son **para** ti.   The flowers are **for** you.

Estamos perdidos **sin** él.   We are lost **without** him.

Queremos ir de vacaciones **con** ustedes. We want to go on vacation **with** you.

In two special cases, when the preposition is "con" and the subject is "mí" or "ti," the preposition and the pronoun are put together to form "conmigo" (with me) and "contigo" (with you).

| ¿Quieres ir al concierto **conmigo**? | Would you like to go to the concert **with me**? |
| No, no puedo ir **contigo** al concierto. | No, I can't go **with you** to the concert. |

When the subject is **él, ellos, ella, ellas, usted, or ustedes**, the prepositional pronoun is **si**, and is usually accompanied by **mismo/a**:

> **Alejandro** es muy egoísta. Siempre habla de **si** mismo.
> **Alejandro** is very conceited. He always talks about **himself.**

Possessive Adjectives and Pronouns

Possessive adjectives and pronouns are used to indicate ownership. When you want to let someone know what's yours, use the following pronouns or adjectives:

STRESSED POSSESSIVE ADJECTIVES

mío/mía	mine	**nuestro/nuestra**	ours
tuyo/tuya	yours	**suyo/suya**	yours (plural),
suyo/suya	his, hers, yours		theirs

UNSTRESSED POSSESSIVE ADJECTIVES

mi	my	**nuestro/a**	our
tu	your	**su**	your (plural)/their
su	his/her/your		

When to use Possessive Adjectives

The first question is "when do you use an unstressed adjective, and when do you use a stressed adjective?" Check out these examples, and then we'll see what the rule is:

| Esta es **mi** casa. | Esta casa es la **mía.** |
| This is **my** house. | This house is **mine.** |

| Aquí está **tu** cartera. | Esta cartera es la **tuya.** |
| Here is **your** wallet. | This wallet is **yours.** |

> **Mi** casa es verde. **Tu** casa es roja. La **mía** es verde.
> La **tuya** es roja.
> **My** house is green. **Your** house is red. **Mine** is
> green. **Yours** is red.

The difference between stressed and unstressed possessive adjectives is emphasis, as opposed to meaning. Saying "this is my house" is not quite as powerful as saying "this house is mine," but both more or less provide the same information. In order to avoid getting confused, just remember that unstressed is the Spanish equivalent of "my" and stressed is the Spanish equivalent of "mine."

In terms of structure, there is an important difference between the two types of adjectives, but it's an easy one to remember: Stressed adjectives come after the noun, but unstressed adjectives come before the noun. Another difference is that while unstressed possessive adjectives agree in number with the noun they describe, stressed possessive adjectives agree in gender and number with the noun they describe. Notice that neither type agrees with the possessor.

If it's not clear to you why these are adjectives when they look so much like pronouns, consider their function. When you say "my house," the noun "house" is being described by "my." I know it seems a bit strange, but any word that describes a noun is an adjective, even if that word looks a lot like a pronoun. The key is how it's being used in the sentence.

POSSESSIVE PRONOUNS
These look like stressed possessive adjectives, but they mean something different. Possessive pronouns <u>replace</u> nouns, they don't <u>describe</u> them.

When to use Possessive Pronouns
This type of pronoun is formed by combining the article of the noun that's being replaced with the appropriate stressed possessive adjective. Just like stressed possessive adjectives, possessive pronouns must agree in gender and number with the nouns they replace.

Mi bicicleta es azul.   **La mía** es azul.
My bicycle is blue.   **Mine** is blue.

Notice how the pronoun not only shows possession, but it also replaces the noun. Here are some more examples:

Mis zapatos son caros.   **Los míos** son caros.
My shoes are expensive.   **Mine** are expensive.

Tu automóvil es rápido.   **El tuyo** es rápido.
Your car is fast.   **Yours** is fast.

No me gustaron los discos que   No me gustaron
ellos trajeron.   **los suyos**.
I didn't like the records they brought.   I didn't like **theirs**.

REFLEXIVE PRONOUNS

Remember those reflexive verbs you saw in the vocabulary review (ponerse, hacerse, etc.)? Those all have a common characteristic, which is that they indicate that the action is being done to or for oneself. When those verbs are conjugated, the reflexive pronoun (which is always "se" in the infinitive) changes according to the subject:

me	myself	**nos**	ourselves
te	yourself	**se**	themselves/
se	him/herself/yourself		yourselves

Reflexive pronouns are used when the subject and indirect object of the sentence are the same. This may sound kind of strange, but after you see some examples it ought to make more sense.

Él **se pone** los pantalones.
He **puts on** (**himself**) the pants.

Ellos **se envuelven** en los asuntos del gobierno.
They **get** (**themselves**) **involved** in government affairs.

Nosotros **nos comemos** la vaca entera.
We (**ourselves**) **eat** the whole cow.

Roberto tiene que **comprarse** una libreta nueva.
Robert needs **to buy** (**himself**) a new notebook.

THE PRONOUN QUE

The pronoun **que** can mean either **who**, **that**, or **which** depending on the context of the sentence. In other words, it can take the place of a person or a thing. Fortunately, it isn't too tough to tell which meaning is correct.

1) ¿Cómo se llama la maestra **que** tuvimos ayer?
   What's the name of the teacher (**who**) we had yesterday?

2) Ése es el equipo **que** más me gusta de todos los demás.
   That's the team (**that/which**) I like more than all the others.

3) ¿Cuál es la revista **que** compraste ayer?
   Which one is the magazine (**that**) you bought yesterday?

In example 1, "que" means "who," since you are talking about a person. In examples 2 and 3, "que" refers to things, so it means "that" or "which."

When to Use Que

Although in English we tend to leave out the pronouns **who**, **that**, and **which**, in Spanish you have to use **que**. **Que** always follows the noun (as in the examples above).

When referring to people, **quien** (or **quienes**) replaces **que** if the pronoun follows a preposition:

El maestro sin **quien** no pudiera haber aprendido el español.
The teacher without **whom** I couldn't have learned Spanish.

Los tipos con **quienes** juego a la pelota.
The fellows with **whom** I play ball.

THE PRONOUN CUAL

Cual (meaning **which** or **what**) is used when a choice is involved. It's used in place of *que* before the verb *ser*, and it has only two forms: singular (**cual**) and plural (**cuales**). Both **cual** and the verb *ser* must agree in number with the thing(s) being asked about:

¿**Cuál** es tu ciudad favorita?   **What** is your favorite city?
¿**Cuáles** son nuestros regalos?   **Which** presents are ours?

DEMONSTRATIVE PRONOUNS AND ADJECTIVES

Demonstrative pronouns have an accent on the first "e." The adjectives don't. First, learn the construction and meaning:

este/esta	this (one)	**estos/estas**	these
ese/esa	that (one)	**esos/esas**	those
aquel/aquella	that (one over there)	**aquellos/aquellas**	those (over there)

ADJECTIVE OR PRONOUN— WHICH IS IT?

If the demonstrative word comes before a noun, then it is an adjective:

Este plato de arroz con pollo es mío.   **This** plate of chicken with rice is mine.

Ese edifício es él de mi hermano.   **That** building is my brother's.

If the demonstrative word takes the place of a noun, then it's a pronoun:

Éste es mío.   **This one** is mine.

Ése es de mi hermano.   **That one** is my brother's.

When used as adjectives, these words mean **this**, **that**, etc. When used as pronouns, they mean **this one**, **that one**, etc. Don't worry about the use of **ese** versus **aquel**. No question on this exam will ask you to pick between the two.

Pronoun Summary

- The types of pronouns that you need to know are subject, object (direct and indirect), possessive, prepositional (which you'll see again later), reflexive, demonstrative, and a couple of odds and ends like **que** and **cual**. We're not guaranteeing that only these types will appear, but if you know these like the back of your hand you should feel confident that you'll be able to tackle most (if not all) of the pronoun questions.

- Don't just memorize what the different pronouns look like! Recognizing them is important, but it's just as important that you understand how and when to use them.

- Don't forget about POE The folks at ETS love to try to trip you up on simple things (like the gender of a pronoun) that are easy to overlook if you're not on your toes. Before you start thinking about grammar on a pronoun question, cancel answers that are wrong based on flagrant stuff like gender, singular vs. plural, etc.

- If all else fails, your ear can sometimes be your guide. In learning Spanish, you probably spoke and heard the language on a pretty regular basis, and so you have a clue as to what correct Spanish sounds like. You don't want to use your ear if you can eliminate answers based on the rules of grammar, but if you've exhausted the rules and you're down to two answers, one of which sounds a lot better than the other, guess the nice-sounding one. The fact is that many grammatical rules were born out of a desire to make the language sound good.

- Last (but not least), don't forget to pace yourself wisely and use the three-pass system. Look for questions that test the pronouns you're most comfortable with, and skip the tough ones. If you're stumped by a question, leave it for the third pass, cancel what you can and guess, but never spend too much time on a question that tests something you don't really know or like.

Pronoun Questions

1) Si el puede hacerlo solo, yo no _____ tengo que ayudar.

   A) la
   B) lo
   C) le
   D) los

2) Pedimos asientos cerca de una ventana, pero _____ dieron éstos.

   A) nos
   B) les
   C) nuestros
   D) me

3) Cuando sus estudiantes se portan mal, la profesora _____ castiga.

   A) las
   B) los
   C) les
   D) le

4) ¿Aquellos guantes que están sobre la butaca son _____?

   A) el mío
   B) de mi
   C) los míos
   D) las mías

5) Por tu cumpleaños _____ daré un caballo nuevo.

   A) le
   B) te
   C) a ti
   D) me

6) ¿_____ es tu cantante favorito?

   A) Quién
   B) Cuál
   C) Quiénes
   D) Qué

7) ¿_____ prefieres? ¿El azul o el rojo?

   A) Qué
   B) Cuál
   C) Cuáles
   D) Ése

Answers and explanations to pronoun questions

1) If he can do it alone, I don't need to help _____.

    A) her
    B) him
    C) to him
    D) them

The direct object of the sentence is **el**, and the correct direct object pronoun for **el** is **lo**.

2) We asked for seats near a window, but they gave _____ these.

    A) to us
    B) to them
    C) ours
    D) to me

Pedimos tells you that the subject of the sentence is **nosotros**. Since you are trying to say "they gave (to) us these," the correct pronoun is **nos** (meaning "to us").

3) When her students misbehave, the professor punishes _____.

    A) them (f)
    B) them (m)
    C) to them
    D) to him

Estudiantes is masculine and plural, so the correct pronoun is **los**. Remember that in Spanish the masculine pronoun is used whenever the gender of a group is mixed even if the majority of the group is female. Also, when the genders of the people in the group are unknown (like in this question) the male pronoun is used.

4) Are those gloves that are on the armchair _____?

    A) mine (m, sing.)
    B) of/about me
    C) mine (m, pl.)
    D) mine (f, pl.)

Guantes is a masculine plural word, so the correct article is **los**. Since you want to say "mine," you would say **los míos**.

5)   For your birthday, I'll give _____ a new horse.

A) to him
B) to you
C) to you
D) to myself

The person whose birthday it is in the sentence is **tu**, so **te** is the correct indirect object pronoun. It is indirect (as opposed to direct) in this case because it takes a preposition (<u>to</u> you I will give...). The reason C is incorrect is because of the placement of the blank. You could (for the sake of emphasis) say "te dare a ti un caballo nuevo," but the pronoun in this case <u>precedes</u> the verb so B is the best answer.

6)   _____ is your favorite singer?

A) Who
B) Which
C) Who (pl.)
D) What

Since the question refers to a single person (el cantante), **quién** is the correct pronoun.

7)   _____ do you prefer? The blue one or the red one?

A) What
B) Which
C) Which (pl.)
D) That one

In this question a choice is being asked for so **cuál** is used instead of **qué**. **Cuáles** is incorrect because the choice is between two singular things.

Verbs

WHAT YOU NEED TO KNOW

You probably learned what felt like a trazillion different verbs and tenses in Spanish class. For the purposes of this test, you only need to know a few of the tenses you learned. What's even better is that you don't need to know how to conjugate verbs in the diferent tenses, nor do you need to know the names for the different tenses. You do need to know how to recognize them. For example, you don't need to know how or why the conditional is used. All you need to know is what it looks like when a verb is in the conditional, and when the conditional is used.

You should focus on recognizing clues (key words, etc.) in the sentences that suggest certain tenses, and then finding the answer in the appropriate tense. Remember, even if you don't know which answer is in the tense that corresponds with the sentence, you can still cancel answers that definitely aren't in that tense. USE POE!! A brief review of the tenses that show up is probably a good place to begin, so let's get right to it.

The Basics: Present, Past, and Future

THE PRESENT TENSE (A.K.A. THE PRESENT INDICATIVE)

The present tense is the easiest, and probably the first tense that you ever learned. It is used when the action is happening in the present, as in the following:

> Yo **hablo** con mis amigos cada día.
> I **speak** with my friends every day.

Since the present is the most basic, and probably the easiest tense to deal with, it rarely shows up as the right answer to a question. So why go over it? Because it sometimes does show up as a right answer, and it often shows up as a wrong answer. You need to know how to recognize it in order to cancel it if it's incorrect. Take a quick glance at the present tenses of the following verbs just to refresh your memory:

	trabajar	**vender**	**escribir**
yo	trabaj**o**	vend**o**	escrib**o**
tú	trabaj**as**	vend**es**	escrib**es**
él/ella	trabaj**a**	vend**e**	escrib**e**
nosotros	trabaj**amos**	vend**emos**	escrib**imos**
ustedes	trabaj**an**	vend**en**	escrib**en**
ellos/ellas	trabaj**an**	vend**en**	escrib**en**

THE PAST TENSE (A.K.A. THE PRETERITE)

The past tense is used to describe an action that had a <u>definite beginning and ending in the past</u> (as opposed to an action that may be ongoing), as in the following example:

> Ayer yo **hablé** con mis amigos.
> Yesterday I **spoke** with my friends.

There are a bunch of different tenses that are "past tenses," that is, that describe actions that took place in the past. There are different tenses for saying "I spoke," "I was speaking," "I have spoken," etc. Let's start by reviewing the most basic of these, the plain past tense:

	trabajar	**vender**	**escribir**
yo	trabaj**é**	vend**í**	escrib**í**
tú	trabaj**aste**	vend**iste**	escrib**iste**
él/ella	trabaj**ó**	vend**ió**	escrib**ió**
nosotros	trabaj**amos**	vend**ímos**	escrib**ímos**
ustedes	trabaj**aron**	vend**ieron**	escrib**ieron**
ellos/ellas	trabaj**aron**	vend**ieron**	escrib**ieron**

The easiest forms to spot are the first and third person singular (**yo** and **él/ella** forms) because of the accent.

THE FUTURE TENSE

The future tense is used to describe things that will <u>definitely</u> happen in the future. The reason we stress "definitely" is that there is a different tense used to describe things that *may* happen in the future. In Spanish, just as in English, there is a difference between being certain (I will go) and being uncertain (I might go), and different tenses are used for the different degrees of certainty. You'll see the fancier stuff later. First take a look at the regular future:

> Mañana yo **hablaré** con mis amigos.
> Tomorrow I **will speak** to my friends.

Notice that what takes two words to say in English (**will speak**) takes only one word to say in Spanish (**hablaré**). The future is a nice, simple tense (no auxiliary verb, only one word) which is easy to spot thanks to the accents that are present and the structure. The future is formed by tacking on the appropriate ending to the infinitive of the verb <u>without dropping the **-ar**, **-er**, or **-ir**</u>.

	trabajar	**vender**	**escribir**
yo	trabajar**é**	vender**é**	escribir**é**
tú	trabajar**ás**	vender**ás**	escribir**ás**
él/ella	trabajar**á**	vender**á**	escribir**á**
nosotros	trabajar**emos**	vender**emos**	escribir**emos**
ustedes	trabajar**án**	vender**án**	escribir**án**
ellos/ellas	trabajar**án**	vender**án**	escribir**án**

The Fancy Stuff

THE PRESENT PERFECT

The present perfect is used to refer to an action that began in the past and is continuing into the present (and possibly beyond). Compare these two sentences:

1)   Ayer **hablé** con mis amigos.
     Yesterday **I spoke** with my friends.

2)   **He hablado** mucho con mis amigos últimamente.
     I have spoken to my friends a lot lately.

The first example is just plain past tense: you started and finished talking with your friends yesterday. In the second example, it's not clear whether you will continue to talk to your friends a lot this week and indefinitely, or whether you will stop speaking to them or speak to them less frequently. In cases like the second example, the present perfect is used. The use of this tense may seem a bit tricky, but if you keep asking yourself whether the action <u>definitely ended</u> in the past, you should be O.K.

Spotting the present perfect is pretty easy. This is a compound tense, meaning that it is formed by combining two verbs. In the present perfect, the two verbs are the present tense of the auxiliary (or helper) verb **haber** and the past participle of the other verb:

	trabajar	**vender**	**escribir**
yo	**he** trabaj**ado**	**he** vend**ido**	**he** esc**rito**
tu	**has** trabaj**ado**	**has** vend**ido**	**has** esc**rito**
el/ella	**ha** trabaj**ado**	**ha** vend**ido**	**ha**esc**rito**
nosotros	**hemos** trabaj**ado**	**hemos** vend**ido**	**hemos** esc**rito**
ustedes	**han** trabaj**ado**	**han** vend**ido**	**han** esc**rito**
ellos/ellas	**han** trabaj**ado**	**han** vend**ido**	**han** esc**rito**

Note: Most past participles are formed by dropping the last two letters from the infinitive and adding **-ido** (for **-er** and **-ir** verbs) or **-ado** (for **-ar** verbs). **Escribir** has an irregular past participle, as do some other verbs, but don't worry about it. This is no problem since the irregulars still look and sound like the regulars, and with respect to this tense you still know it's the present perfect because of **haber**.

THE IMPERFECT

The imperfect is yet another past tense used to describe actions that occurred continuously in the past, but are no longer occurring. This is different from the preterite, which describes "one-time" actions that began and ended in the past. Look at the two side by side and the difference will become clearer:

Ayer **yo hablé** con mis amigos.

Yo hablaba con mis amigos cada día.

Yesterday **I spoke** with my friends.

I used to speak with my friends each day.

"I used to speak . . ." implies that you no longer speak with your friends each day.

Even though the action has ended, when it was happening it was a repeated event, so the imperfect is used.

The imperfect is also used to describe conditions or circumstances in the past:

Era una noche oscura y tormentosa.
It was a dark and stormy night.

Cuando **tenía** diez años . . .
When **I was** ten years old . . .

Make sense? Good, now check out the formation:

	trabajar	**vender**	**escribir**
yo	trabaj**aba**	vend**ía**	escrib**ía**
tú	trabaj**abas**	vend**ías**	escrib**ías**
él/ella	trabaj**aba**	vend**ía**	escrib**ía**
nosotros	trabaj**ábamos**	vend**íamos**	escrib**íamos**
ustedes	trabaj**aban**	vend**ían**	escrib**ían**
ellos/ellas	trabaj**aban**	vend**ían**	escrib**ían**

Although the imperfect is sort of close to the other past tenses you've seen (i.e., the preterite and the present perfect) in terms of usage, it looks different from the present perfect. That's the key since half of your job is just to know what the different tenses look like. To keep them clear in your mind, remember that the present perfect is compound (so it uses two verbs). The toughest part will be distinguishing the preterite from the imperfect. You've just got to memorize them.

Back to The Future: The Conditional

Remember the future tense? (It's the one that's used to describe actions that are *definitely* going to happen in the future.) Well now you'll learn the other future tense you will need to know, the one that's used to describe things that *may* happen in the future.

The conditional describes what could, would, or might happen in the future:

Me **gustaría** hablar con mis amigos cada día.
I **would like** to talk to my friends each day.

Con más tiempo, **podría** hablar con ellos el día entero.
With more time, I **could** speak with them all day long.

Si gasto cinco pesos, solamente me **quedarán** tres.
If I spend five dollars, I **would** only **have** three (left).

It can also be used to make a request in a softer way:

¿**Puedes** prestar atención?	¿**Podrías** prestar atención?
Can you pay attention?	**Could you** pay attention?

The conditional is formed by taking the future stem of the verb (which is usually the infinitive) and adding the conditional ending:

	escribir	**trabajar**	**vender**
yo	escribir**ía**	trabajar**ía**	vender**ía**
tú	escribir**ías**	trabajar**ías**	vender**ías**
él/ella	escribir**ía**	trabajar**ía**	vender**ía**
nosotros	escribir**íamos**	trabajar**íamos**	vender**íamos**
ustedes	escribir**ían**	trabajar**ían**	vender**ían**
ellos/ellas	escribir**ían**	trabajar**ían**	vender**ían**

To avoid confusing the conditional with the future, concentrate on the conditional endings. The big difference is the accented **í** that is in the conditional, but not in the future:

FUTURE	**CONDITIONAL**
trabajaré	trabajaría
venderán	venderían
escribiremos	escribiríamos

THE SUBJUNCTIVE
Don't give up now! Just two more verb tenses (the present subjunctive and the imperfect subjunctive) and you'll be done with all this verb business (give or take a couple of special topics).

THE PRESENT SUBJUNCTIVE
When you want to tell someone what to do in Spanish (i.e., give a command), you have to use the present subjunctive:

¡No **hables** con tus amigos!   ¡**Hablen** con sus amigos!
Don't **speak** with your friends!   **Speak** with your (pl) friends!

Commands can also be given indirectly:

Quiero que **hablen** con sus amigos.
I want you to **speak** with your friends.

This is called an indirect command because the person being bossed around is not the subject of the sentence. In Spanish, the same tense (the present subjunctive) is used for both types of commands.

The present subjunctive is also used when a wish or desire is involved:

Quiero que **comas** los vegetales.
I want you **to eat** the vegetables.

Pido que me **acompañes** a la oficina del médico.
I'm asking you **to accompany** me to the doctor's
    office.

Espero que la lluvia **pare** antes del comienzo del
    juego.
I hope the rain **stops** before the beginning of the game.

The subjunctive is formed by taking the **yo** form of the present tense, dropping the -**o**, and adding the appropriate ending:

	trabajar	**vender**	**escribir**
yo	trabaj**e**	vend**a**	escrib**a**
tú	trabaj**es**	vend**as**	escrib**as**
él/ella	trabaj**e**	vend**a**	escrib**a**
nosotros	trabaj**emos**	vend**amos**	escrib**amos**
ustedes	trabaj**en**	vend**an**	escrib**an**
ellos/ellas	trabaj**en**	vend**an**	escrib**an**

The one exception to this happens in the *tú* form of affirmative commands, which have special endings:

¡Trabaj**a** con tu padre!   ¡Vend**e** el carro!   ¡Escrib**e** la carta!

The present subjunctive is easy to spot because certain clue phrases will tell you that a wish or desire is happening. Look for **quiero que, pido que, espero que, dudo que, etc**. Basically, any expression of doubt or emotion (as well as direct and indirect commands) requires the subjunctive.

THE IMPERFECT SUBJUNCTIVE

Here we are, at the final verb tense you'll need to know for the SAT!! This version of the subjunctive is used with the same expressions as the present subjunctive (doubt, emotion, fear), but it's used when you're in the past:

Quería que **comieras** los vegetales.
I wanted you **to eat** the vegetables.

Pedía que me **acompañaras** a la oficina del médico.
I asked that you **accompany** me to the doctor's office.

Esperaba que la lluvia **parara** antes del comienzo del
    juego.
I hoped that the rain **would stop** before the beginning
    of the game.

One very important thing to notice in the examples above is that it's the <u>expression</u> being in the past that suggests that you use the imperfect subjunctive. If you're looking at a sentence that you know takes the subjunctive, but you're not sure whether it's present or imperfect, focus on the expression. If the expression is in the present, use the present subjunctive. If the expression is in the past, use the imperfect subjunctive.

The imperfect subjunctive is formed by taking the *ellos/ellas* form of the preterite (which you already know, right?) and adding the correct ending:

	trabajar	**vender**	**escribir**
yo	trabajar**a**	vendier**a**	escribier**a**
tú	trabajar**as**	vendier**as**	escribier**as**
él/ella	trabajar**a**	vendier**a**	escribier**a**
nosotros	trabajár**amos**	vendiér**amos**	escribiér**amos**
ustedes	trabajar**an**	vendier**an**	escribier**an**
ellos/ellas	trabajar**an**	vendier**an**	escribier**an**

Verbs that are in the imperfect subjunctive shouldn't be too tough to spot when they show up in the answer choices. It has almost completely different endings from the preterite. It's not a compound tense, so you won't confuse it with the present perfect. The stems are different from the present subjunctive, so distinguishing between those two shouldn't be a problem.

Okay, there is some slightly bad news— it's almost exactly like the imperfect. There is a difference though, and it's in the stem. Don't try to tell the difference by looking at the endings, because there isn't one. Compare the same verb in the imperfect and the imperfect subjunctive:

imperfect	vs.	imperfect
		subjunctive
trabaja**ba**		trabaja**ra**
vend**ías**		vend**ieras**
escrib**ímos**		escrib**iéramos**

Special Topics

SER VS. ESTAR

The verbs **ser** and **estar** both mean "to be" when translated into English. If you weren't aware of this, turn back to the vocabulary review to refresh your memory. You might wonder "why is it necessary to have two verbs that mean exactly the same thing?" Good question. The answer is that in Spanish, unlike in English, there is a distinction between temporary states of being (e.g., I am hungry) and fixed, or permanent states of being (e.g., I am Cuban). Although this difference seems pretty simple and easy to follow, there are some cases when it isn't so clear. Consider the following examples:

> El señor González _____ mi doctor.
> Cynthia _____ mi novia.

Would you use **ser** or **estar** in these two sentences? After all, Cynthia may or may not be your girlfriend forever, and the same goes for Mr. González's status as your doctor. You might get rid of both of them tomorrow (or one of them might get rid of you)! So which verb do you use?

In both cases, the answer is **ser**, because in both cases there is no foreseeable end to the relationships described. In other words, even though they may change, nothing in either sentence gives any reason to think they will. So whether you and Cynthia go on to marry or she dumps you tomorrow, you would be correct if you used **ser**. When in doubt, ask yourself "does this action/condition have a definite end in the near or immediate future?" If so, use **estar**. Otherwise, use **ser**. Try the following drill:

Fill the blank with the correct form of **ser** or **estar**.

1) Pablo _____ muy cansado.
2) El automóvil _____ roto.
3) No puedo salir de casa esta noche porque _____castigado.
4) Mi hermano _____ muy gracioso.
5) Mis profesores _____ demasiado serios.
6) Ayer salí sin abrigo, y pues hoy _____ enfermo.
7) Los tacos que mi madre cocina _____ ricos.
8) No podemos empezar! Todavía no _____ listos.
9) _____ muy bravo con el tipo que me insultó.

Answers: 1) está 2) está 3) estoy 4) es 5) son 6) estoy
           7) son 8) estamos 9) estuve

Don't assume that certain adjectives (like *enfermo*, for example) necessarily take **estar**. If you're saying someone is sick as in a cold, then **estar** is appropriate. If you're saying that someone is sick as in demented, then **ser** is correct.

Unfortunately, usage is not the only tough thing about these two verbs. They are both irregular, and they come up all over this exam. Spend a little time reviewing the conjugations of **ser** and **estar** before you move on:

estar
present: estoy, estás, está, estamos, están, están
preterite: estuve, estuviste, estuvo, estuvimos, estuvieron, estuvieron
pres. subj.: esté, estés, esté, estemos, estén, estén
imp. subj.:   estuviera, estuvieras, estuviera, estuviéramos, estuvieran, estuvieran

The other tenses of **estar** follow the regular patterns for **-ar** verbs.

ser
present: soy, eres, es, somos, son, son
imperfect: era, eras, era, éramos, eran, eran
preterite: fui, fuiste, fue, fuimos, fueron, fueron
pres. subj.: sea, seas, sea, seamos, sean, sean
imp. subj.:   fuera, fueras, fuera, fuéramos, fueran, fueran

The other tenses of **ser** follow the regular patterns for -er verbs.

CONOCER VS. SABER

We hate to do this to you again, but there is another pair of verbs that have the same English translations but are used differently in Spanish. However, don't worry: these two have (mostly) regular conjugations, and knowing when to use them is really very straightforward.

The words **conocer** and **saber** both mean "to know." In Spanish, knowing a person or a thing (basically, a noun) is different from knowing a piece of information. Compare the uses of **conocer** and **saber** in these sentences:

¿**Sabes** cuanto cuesta la camisa?
Do you know how much the shirt costs?

¿**Conoces** a mi primo?
Do you know my cousin?

Sabemos que Pelé fue un gran futbolista.
We know that Pelé was a great soccer player.

Conocemos a Pelé.
We know Pelé.

When what's known is a person, place, or thing, use **conocer**. When what's known is a fact, use **saber**. The same basic rule holds for questions:

¿**Saben** a qué hora llega el presidente?
Do you know what time the president arrives?

¿**Conocen** al presidente?
Do you know the president?

Now that you know how they're used, take a look at their conjugations:

<u>conocer</u>
present: conozco, conoces, conoce, conocemos,
              conocen, conocen
pres. subj.: conozca, conozcas, conozca,
              conozcamos, conozcan, conozcan

The other tenses of **conocer** follow the regular **-er** pattern.

saber
present: sé, sabes, sabe, sabemos, saben, saben
preterite: supe, supiste, supo, supimos, supieron, supieron
future: sabré, sabrás, sabrá, sabremos, sabrán, sabrán
conditional: sabría, sabrías, sabría, sabríamos, sabrían, sabrían
pres. subj.: sepa, sepas, sepa, sepamos, sepan, sepan
imp. subj.: supiera, supieras, supiera, supiéramos, supieran, supieran

In the following drill, fill in the blanks with the correct form of **conocer** or **saber**:

1) ¡Él _____ cocinar muy bien!
2) ¿_____ el libro que ganó el premio? (tú)
3) Las mujeres _____ bailar como si juesen profesionales.
4) ¡¿Es verdad que _____ a Michael Jackson?! (ustedes)
5) Es importante _____ nadar.
6) No _____ como voy a ganar la carrera.
7) ¿Cómo puede ser que tú no _____ la casa donde viviste?
8) Los dos abogados no se _____ uno al otro porque nunca han trabajado juntos.
9) _____ que vamos a divertirnos en el circo esta noche. (yo)

Answers: 1) sabe 2) conoces 3) saben 4) conocen
          5) saber 6) sé 7) conoces 8) conocen 9) Sé

Verb Summary

- The tenses you need to know are the present, past, future, conditional, imperfect, present perfect, and subjunctive (both present and imperfect). In terms of memorizing and reviewing them, we think the best approach is to lump them together in the following way:

Present Tenses	Past Tenses	Future Tenses
Present	Past	Future
Present Subjunctive	Imperfect	Conditional
Present Perfect	Imperfect Subjunctive	

By thinking in terms of these groupings, you'll find that eliminating answers is a snap once you've determined the tense of the sentence. That is your first step on a question that is testing your knowledge of verb tenses: determine the tense of the sentence (or at least whether it's a "past," "present," or "future" tense), and cancel.

- When memorizing the uses of the different tenses, focus on clues that point to one tense or another:

  - There are certain expressions (fear, doubt, emotion) that tell you to use the subjunctive, and whether the expression is in the present or the past will tell you which subjunctive to use.

  - To distinguish between future and conditional, focus on the certainty of the event's occurrence.

  - The three past tenses are differentiated by the end (or lack thereof) of the action and when that end occurred. If the action had a clear beginning and ending in the past, use the regular past. If the action was continuing in the past, but is no longer happening use the imperfect. If the action began in the past and is continuing into the present, use the present perfect.

    - Recognizing the different tenses shouldn't be too tough if you focus on superficial characteristics.

    - The only compound tense you're likely to see is the present perfect.

- Certain tenses have accents, others do not.

• As far as pacing goes, apply the same principles that we outlined for pronoun questions: spend time on the easy ones and use POE and guess on the tougher ones. Keep in mind that although the simple tenses (present, past, and future) do appear, they are seldom the correct answer. Why? Because they're the first tenses you learned, they're the easiest to use, and the test writers know that you'll guess them if you're stuck on a question. They don't want you to guess successfully, so they use these basic tenses as trap answers. Careful now, we didn't say they were never right, only seldom.

Verb Questions

1) Cuando tenga dinero, te _____ un automóvil de lujo.

   A) compraré
   B) compre
   C) compraría
   D) compraste

2) Quiero que _____ la tarea antes de acostarte.

   A) hiciste
   B) hace
   C) haga
   D) hagas

3) El año pasado nosotros _____ a México para las vacaciones.

   A) iremos
   B) fuimos
   C) iríamos
   D) vamos

4) Si tuvieran tiempo, _____ pasar el tiempo relajando.

   A) quieren
   B) querían
   C) quieran
   D) quisieran

5) Esperaba que ustedes _____ a construir el barco.

   A) ayudarían
   B) ayudaran
   C) ayudaron
   D) ayudan

6) Carlos _____ mucho tiempo estudiando la biología ultimamente.

   A) paso
   B) pasaría
   C) pasaba
   D) ha pasado

Answers and explanations to verb questions

1) When I have money, _____ (for) you a luxury car.

   A) will buy (future)
   B) bought (past- yo form)
   C) would buy (conditional)
   D) bought (past- tu form)

The sentence refers to something that will happen in the future, so the correct answer will either be in the future or the conditional. In this case the event is certain (I will buy you a luxury car), therefore the future is correct.

2) I want you to _____ the homework before going to bed.

   A) did (past- tu form)
   B) does (present- el form)
   C) do (present subjunctive- el form)
   D) do (present subjunctive- tu form)

Quiero que is one of those expressions that tells you to use the subjunctive. In this case the expression is in the present tense so the present subjunctive is correct. If the expression were in the past (queria que) you'd use the imperfect subjunctive. The reason D is correct is that **tu** is the dir. obj. pronoun in the sentence, so you want the **tu** form of the verb.

3) Last year we _____ to Mexico for vacation.

   A) will go (future)
   B) went (past)
   C) would go (conditional)
   D) go (present)

El año pasado (last year) is a big hint that the answer will be some kind of past tense. Since the event had a definite beginning and end in the past, the regular past tense is correct.

4) If they had time, they _____ to pass the time relaxing.

   A) want to (present)
   B) wanted to (imperfect)
   C) want to (present subjunctive)
   D) would want to (conditional)

Si tuvieran tells you to use the conditional (in fact, **si** often precedes use of the conditional because it introduces a condition that doesn't currently exist). The only answer that's in the conditional is **quisieran**.

5) I expected that you _____ build the boat.

   A) would help (conditional)
   B) would have helped (imperfect subjunctive)
   C) helped (past)
   D) help (present)

Esperaba que is another one of those expressions of emotion that tell you to use the subjunctive, but this time around the expression is in the past so the correct tense is the imperfect subjunctive. Remember, the tense of the expression or emotion is what tells you whether to use the present or the imperfect subjunctive.

6) Carlos _____ much time studying biology lately.

   A) spent (past)
   B) would spend (conditional)
   C) spent (imperfect)
   D) has spent (present perfect)

Although the present perfect is a compound tense (that is, it takes a helper verb), this actually makes it easiest to spot because it stands out. In this sentence it is correct because the action began in the past and is possibly continuing into the present.

PREPOSITIONS

Prepositions are those little words that show the relationship between two other words. In English, they're words like to, from, at, for, about, etc. In Spanish they're words like **a, de, sobre,** etc.

Part of what you need to know about prepositions is what the different ones mean. That's the easy part. The other thing you need to know is how and when to use them. You need to know which verbs and expressions take prepositions and which prepositions they take. This isn't too terrible to learn either, but it can be tricky if you rely too heavily on your ear:

Trata de comer más vegetales.

Uno debe tratar a los profesores con respeto.

El libro trata de un general famoso.

See what we mean? Some verbs and expressions don't always take the same preposition so you'll have to memorize the different possibilities and how to spot them.

NOW FOR THE GOOD NEWS

The good news is that ETS only likes to test a very small number of prepositions so you can limit your study to those instead of trying to master every preposition in existence. Yes, it is a lot like doing vocabulary work, but once again you probably already know many of these expressions so it shouldn't be too terrible.

MORE GOOD NEWS

Remember the beginning of this chapter, when you learned that part of part A of the exam would focus on grammar instead of meaning, and that meant the answer choices on a given question would mean roughly the same thing? Well, we lied (sort of), but that's actually a good thing. What we're getting at is that with preposition questions (unlike verb and pronoun questions) in part B the answers sometimes do have different meanings, and this makes POE a lot easier.

COMMON PREPOSITIONS AND THEIR USES

a: to

Vamos a la obra de teatro esta noche?
Are we going to the play tonight?

de: of

Son las gafas de mi hermano.
Those are my brother's glasses (literally "the glasses of my
    brother").

con: with

Me gusta mucho el arroz con pollo.
I like chicken with rice a lot.

sobre: on; about; over

Los vaqueros se montaran sobre el caballo.
The cowboys got on the horse.

Esta semana gané veinte pesos sobre lo que gané la semana
    pasada.
This week I earned twenty dollars over what I earned last week.

Los señores hablaron sobre la situación en Cuba.
The men talked about the situation in Cuba.

antes de: before

Antes de salir quiero ponerme un sombrero.
Before going out I want to put on a hat.

despues de: after

Despues de comer me gusta caminar un poco.
After eating I like to take a short walk.

en: in

Regresan en una hora.
They'll be back in an hour.

Alguien está en el baño.
Someone is in the bathroom.

entre: between

La carnicería está entre la pescadería y el cine.
The butcher shop is between the fish store and the movie house.

La conferencia duro entre dos y tres horas.
The conference lasted between two and three hours.

durante: during

Durante el verano me gusta nadar cada día.
During the summer I like to swim each day.

desde: since; from

Desde que tenía diez años he tomado vitaminas.
Since I was ten years old I've been taking vitamins.

Se pueden ver las montañas desde aquí.
The mountains can be seen from here.

PARA VS. POR

The prepositions **para** and **por** both mean "for" (as well as other things depending on context) but they are used for different situations, and so they tend to cause a bit of confusion. Luckily there are some pretty clear-cut rules as to when you use **para** and when you use **por**, because they both tend to sound fine even when they're being used incorrectly. Try to avoid using your ear when choosing between these two.

When to use para

The following are examples of the most common situations in which **para** is used. Instead of memorizing some stuffy rule, we suggest that you get a feel for what types of situations imply the use of **para**, so that when you see those situations come up on your SAT you'll recognize them.

to express opinion . . .

Para mi, el lunes es el día mas largo de la semana.
In my opinion (literally "for me"), Monday is the longest
    day of the week.

to express purpose . . .

El regalo es **para** ti.
The gift is for you.

No comas el helado! Es **para** tu fiesta mañana.
Don't eat the ice cream! It's for your party tomorrow.

to qualify or offer a point of reference . . .

Para un niño joven, tiene muchísimo talento.
For a young kid, he's got loads of talent.

When to use por

Por can mean simply for, but it can also mean by, in exchange for, around, as a substitute for, etc. Study the following possibilities and you should have all the bases covered.

to express a period of time . . .

Trabajé con el instituto durante quince años.
I worked with the institute for fifteen years.

to express how you got somewhere . . . (by)

Fuimos a Italia **por** barco.
We went to Italy by boat.

Pasamos **por** esa tienda ayer cuando salimos del pueblo.
We passed by that store yesterday when we left the town.

to describe a trade . . . (in exchange for)

Te cambiaré mi automóvil **por** el tuyo este fin de semana.
I'll give you my car for yours this weekend.

to lay blame or identify cause . . . (by)

Todos los barcos fueron destruidos **por** la tormenta.
All the boats were destroyed by the storm.

to identify gain or motive . . . (for; as a substitute for)

Ella hace todo lo posible **por** su hermana.
She does all she can for her sister.

Cuando Arsenio está enfermo, su madre trabaja **por** él.
When Arsenio is ill, his mother works (as a substitute) for him.

TWO FREQUENTLY USED PREPOSITIONAL PHRASES: "IR A" AND "ACABAR DE"

Ir a is used to describe what the future will bring, or in other words, what is going to happen. The expression is formed by combining the appropriate form of **ir** in the present tense (subject and verb must agree) with the preposition **a**:

Mañana **vamos a** comprar el árbol de Navidad.
Tomorrow we are going to buy the Christmas tree.
¿**Vas a** la escuela incluso si te sientes mal?
You're going to school even if you feel ill?

Acabar de is basically the Spanish equivalent of just, and is used to talk about what just happened. It is formed just like **ir a**, with the appropriate form of **acabar** in the present tense followed by **de**:

Acabo de terminar decocinar el pavo.
I just finished cooking the turkey.

Ellos **acaban de** regresar del mercado.
They just got back from the supermarket.

Other prepositions and prepositional phrases you should know (Notice that many of these are merely adverbs with **a** or **de** tacked on to the end to make them prepositions.)

hacia	towards
enfrente de	in front of
frente a	in front of
dentro de	inside of
fuera de	outside of
a la derecha de	to the right of
a la izquierda de	to the left of
debajo de	underneath
encima de	above, on top of
alrededor de	around, surrounding
en medio de	in the middle of
hasta	until
tras	behind
cerca de	near to
lejos de	far from
detras de	behind

delante de	in front of
al lado de	next to
junto a	near to, close to
a tiempo	on time
a fondo	thorough
por regla general	as a rule, in general
con profundidad	profoundly
por eso	that's why
al llegar	upon arriving
trabajar de	to work as
ver a	to see . . .
tener frio en	to be cold in
en el periodico	in the newspaper
de buena gana	willfully
en marcha	on the move
con disgusto	with disgust
para ir a	in order to get to
entrar a	to go into
salir de	to come out of
ponerse a	to make oneself or put oneself
en el suelo	on the floor
servir a	to serve . . .
vestido de	dressed as
dirigirse a	to address (as in speak to)
oir a	to hear . . .
comprar a	to buy . . .
la hora de	the hour to
quejarse a	to complain to
cantidad de	amount of
ponerle fin a	to put a stop to
venir a	to come to
de lujo	expensive (literally "of luxury")
lleno de	full of
reirse de	to laugh at
de origen humilde	of humble beginnings
encontrar a	to find . . .
mimar a	to spoil, indulge . . .
pedir que	to ask that
pedir a	to ask for
en vez de	instead of
a mediados de	midway through
viajar en	to travel in
tocar a	to touch . . .
a la vista	visible, within view

Preposition Summary

- Much of your work with prepositions boils down to memorization: which expressions and verbs go with which prepositions, etc. Keep in mind the big picture, which is that preposition questions account for less than fifteen percent of the questions on part A of your exam, so don't drive yourself nuts trying to memorize every single one you've ever heard.

- First off, you should concentrate on the bold-faced examples at the beginning of the "Preposition" section because those are the most common. Once you're comfortable with them, the subsequent list should be a snap because many of those expressions are merely adverbs with **a** or **de** after them.

- Some verbs take prepositions all the time, some never do, and others sometimes do. This isn't as confusing as it may sound though, because the different prepositions (or lack thereof) will change the meanings of the verbs; so if you know what you're trying to say you just have to make sure you tack on the preposition that means the proper thing. Consider the following:

  Voy a tratar _____ despertarme más temprano.
  A) a
  B) de
  C) con
  D) sin

  Which one of these goes with tratar?! Well actually, each of them could depending on what you were trying to say. In this case you want to say "try to," so **de** is the appropriate preposition. **Tratar a** means "to treat," **tratar con** means "to deal with," and **tratar sin** means "to try without." None of them makes sense in this sentence. The moral of the story is don't try to memorize which verbs go with which prepositions, concentrate on meaning.

- Just like you did with the vocabulary list, scan the prepositional phrase list and check off the expressions you are comfortable with and certain that you'll remember on the day of the exam. You may want to briefly review them closer to the date of the test, but for now focus your efforts on what you have trouble with.

Preposition Questions

1)   Quiero llegar a la fiesta antes _____ María.

   A) de
   B) de que
   C) a
   D) sin

2)   Todos mis alumnos estuvieron _____ acuerdo
   conmigo.

   A) entre
   B) en
   C) con
   D) de

3)   Estamos apurados, y por eso tenemos que viajar
   _____ el camino más corto.

   A) dentro de
   B) por
   C) alrededor de
   D) para

4)   Los paraguas se usan _____ parar la lluvia.

   A) en medio de
   B) hacia
   C) para
   D) por

5)   La próxima semana ellos van _____ tocar aquí.

   A) a
   B) de
   C) con
   D) por

6)   No me gusta ver las películas de horror _____
   la noche.

   A) tras de
   B) sobre
   C) en
   D) durante

7)   Salieron hace un rato, así que deben regresar
   _____ cinco minutos.

   A) alrededor de
   B) en vez de
   C) en
   D) despues de

Answers and Explanations to Preposition Questions

1) I want to arrive at the party _____ Maria.

   A) before
   B) before that . . .
   C) before at
   D) before without

In the original sentence you're given antes followed by a blank, leaving it up to you to fill in the correct preposition. Antes tells you that the meaning you're going for is "before," so **de** is the correct preposition. Choice B (**antes de que**) is one of those expressions that would need to be followed by a verb in the imperfect. The others are way off in terms of meaning.

2) All of the students were _____ agreement with me.

   A) between
   B) in
   C) with
   D) of

This is a tough question, especially if you haven't seen the expression **estar de acuerdo**. In English we say that two people are in agreement with each other, but unfortunately the Spanish translation isn't the literal equivalent of the English expression. In Spanish two people **estan de acuerdo**. (We know this isn't on your list, but that list is only a start: if you find new expressions that you don't know, add to your list!)

3) We're in a rush, so we must travel _____ the shortest route.

   A) inside of
   B) by
   C) around
   D) for

This is the old **para** vs. **por** trap, which is definitely tricky. In this case you want to say "travel by," and **por** is the preposition that sometimes means by. **Para** is never used to mean "by."

4) Umbrellas are used _____ stopping the rain.

    A) in the middle of
    B) towards
    C) for
    D) for

Here it is again, **para** vs. **por**. The other choices are pretty clearly wrong based on meaning, which leaves us with C and D. In what sense are we saying "for" in this sentence? Is it "for the purpose of " (which would tell you to use **para**) or "for" as in a period of time or cause of action (which would tell you to use **por**)? In this case "for the purpose of " fits pretty neatly, and so **para** is correct.

5) Next week they are going _____ play here.

    A) to
    B) of
    C) with
    D) for

Nice and easy, no tricks or traps, and it translates straight from English. This is an example of the use of **ir a**. Notice that **ir** is conjugated to agree with the subject of the sentence (ellos).

6) I don't like to see horror films _____ the night.

    A) behind
    B) on
    C) in
    D) during

Pretty tough call between C and D because both sound fine in the blank, but one of them makes a little more sense than the other if you think carefully about the difference in meaning between the two. Do you see films in (like inside) the night, or during the night? They're sort of close, but during makes a bit more sense.

7) They went out a while ago, so they should return _____ five minutes.

    A) around
    B) instead of
    C) in
    D) after

Basically what you're trying to say is that they'll be back soon, and "in five minutes" says that. "Around" would be fine if it were preceded by "in," or if "from now" were tacked on to the end of the sentence, but neither is the case here. Choices B and D don't really make sense.

CHAPTER FIVE

Paragraph Completion

Congratulations! If you've made it this far, that means you've completed the review of all the grammar and vocabulary that's likely to appear on your SST! No more new material (although it would probably be wise to continue reviewing anything that gave you trouble up to now). Now all that's left for you to do is learn the best ways to approach the two remaining question types: Reading Comprehension and Paragraph Completion. In this chapter you'll learn about part B of your exam, Paragraph Completion. First, read the directions:

<u>Directions:</u> Each of the following passages contains numbered blanks indicating that words or phrases have been omitted from the text. First, read quickly thorugh the entire passage to determine its general meaning. Then read it a second time. For each numbered blank, choose the completion that is most appropriate given the context of the entire passage and fill in the corresponding oval on the answer sheet.

Part B is a lot like a combination of parts vocabulary and grammar sentence completion. You're given two to four (most likely three) brief paragraphs (roughly five to seven sentences each) with several words or phrases replaced by blanks. Your job is to fill the blanks with the answers that are appropriate based on either meaning or grammar. How do you know whether it's a "meaning" blank or a "grammar" blank? Well, if it's a grammar blank the answers will all have the same (or very similar) meanings and you'll have to choose based on form or verb tense. Sound familiar? It should since it's the same as part A. The meaning-blank answers will have different meanings, only one of which will make sense in the context of the passage. These questions are just like those in part A.

So what's the difference between parts A and B? In part A, if a sentence makes no sense you just skip it and go on to the next one—no sweat. In part B, missing a sentence is a bit more important since it could make understanding the overall passage a bit tough. You don't need to get every single word, but getting at least the gist of each of the sentences is definitely helpful.

What You Need to Know

As we mentioned earlier, you've already covered the material necessary to answer the questions in part B. The vocabulary is all you need for the meaning questions, and the grammar (especially verb tenses) is all you need for the grammar questions. This does not mean you're ready to do drills! First you need to learn the best way to approach the overall section.

PACING

Since the passages in part B have different degrees of difficulty, but are in no particular order, your first decision is the order in which to attack these questions. As in part A, you want to start with the easiest questions and finish up with the toughest ones. In part B this decision will be more involved and more important, because if you choose to do a really tough passage first this will probably waste time and could throw off your pacing on the remainder of the section. We're not trying to make it sound like life or death. We're just saying that by taking on these passages in the proper order you can make the section easier for yourself. You're going to do all three, but you're going to do them in the order that you like, NOT the order that ETS likes.

Your decision should be based on a brief skim of the first couple of sentences of the passage. If these sentences make sense, and the writing style strikes you as being pretty clear, go for it. If you have any doubt as to whether this passage is going to be easy, go on and see what the next one looks like. Your goal is to find the easiest one and to do it first.

<u>Don't base your decision on subject matter</u>. The fact that a passage is about something you know about or find interesting doesn't mean much if you can't understand every third word. You're not going to be asked about content (that comes later in the reading comprehension), you'll only be asked to fill in blanks. That means that you don't need to retain the information in the passage, but that you need to understand the tense that it's in and the meaning of individual sentences. In other words, topic doesn't count for much. Base your decision on writing style and vocabulary.

Three-Pass System

Once you've decided which passage you're doing first, what next? Next you're going to answer the questions, but once again you'll do them in the order that's best for you.

FIRST PASS

The questions on each of the part B passages should roughly be done in order. In other words, start at the beginning. It'll give you some sense of the passage's structure, which will probably make you more comfortable with it overall. On the other hand, on your first pass through the passage you should skip any question that looks like it even <u>might</u> be tricky. Attempt only the very easiest questions on this pass. Focus on the ones you know the answer to without using POE or anything else but your knowledge of the grammar or vocabulary.

SECOND PASS

On the second pass you'll start using POE to eliminate and guess. Go back to the ones you left blank on the first pass and see if there are any answers that can be eliminated. Don't go in looking for the right answer. Instead, look to cancel wrong answers. You'll find (just as you did on part A) that some of the wrong answers are pretty obviously wrong, and in some cases you'll be able to cancel all but one—the right one.

Don't be intimidated if the sentence that contains a certain blank is difficult. You can determine what tense a verb is in even if you don't understand the verb's meaning! The same goes for pronouns and prepositions. If you are pretty sure that the noun that's being replaced is feminine (e.g., the noun ends in an -**a**), then cancel those masculine pronouns! You have to be aggressive if you want to take advantage of POE

As far as "meaning" blanks are concerned, use the same technique you learned for second-pass questions on part A. Piece together any words in the sentence that you know to try to get some sense of the context. See if any of the answers are completely wacky based on that context. This is where a general knowledge of the passage can be helpful to you as well. Any sentence in the passage, even if you don't understand it, has to make sense within the topic and intention of the overall passage. In other words, there won't be a sentence about the history of the toothpick in a passage about military strategies. Answer choices that seem to stray off the subject of the overall passage are probably wrong.

THIRD PASS

As before, spend very little time, cancel what you can based on whatever clues the sentence or passage has to offer, use your ear if necessary, and guess. The same rule about not guessing holds here as well. If you can't cancel any of the answers, then it's fine to leave a question blank.

It's very easy to fall into a mind-set that says you're not done with a passage until every single question is answered, but this is a dangerous mind-set. Just because a passage is easy overall, that doesn't mean every single question in that passage is a gift.

Don't waste your time: if you've answered all the questions that you can and there are still one or two blank, move on to the next passage. You may never have to, but you should be prepared to skip some questions.

Summary

- This section is just a combination of the two that preceded it. You should be warmed up and confident going in. No new information, just a different format.

- The majority of the blanks will test you on meaning. If the answer to a meaning question isn't immediately apparent, leave it for the second pass. When you come back to it, try to determine the context of the sentence and use POE

- Determine passage order—this could make the difference between smooth sailing and a really big headache, so don't rush your decision.

- Use the Three-Pass System: do easy questions first, tougher questions second, and cancel what you can and guess on whatever's left.

- Don't feel as if you have to answer every single question on a given passage. Sometimes your best move is to go on to the next passage.

Practice Questions

PART B

> **Directions:** Each of the following passages contains numbered blanks indicating that words or phrases have been omitted from the text. First, read quickly thorugh the entire passage to determine its general meaning. Then read it a second time. For each numbered blank, choose the completion that is most appropriate given the context of the entire passage and fill in the corresponding oval on the answer sheet.

Parecía que el pasado 6 de abril todo __(1)__ listo para el despegue del transbordador Discovery cuya misión era la de realizar investigaciones atmosféricas y __(2)__ solares, pero un __(3)__ de última hora obligó a la Agencia Nacional de

Aeronáutica y el Espacio (NASA) a abortar por __(4)__ vez consecutiva el lanzamiento de la nave.

Al cierre de esta edición, la causa del incidente aún era desconocida y se esperaba que el viaje espacial pudiera concretarse __(5)__ cualquier momento.

El apagado del motor ocurrió __(6)__ antes de que los tres motores principales de la nave, alimentados por hidrógeno, fueran activados a las 2:32 de la __(7)__ del pasado 6 de abril, unos 6.6 segundos antes del lanzamiento.

1. A) estaba
   B) esté
   C) estaría
   D) está

2. A) clases
   B) estudios
   C) cuentos
   D) lecturas

3. A) negocio
   B) testigo
   C) retrato
   D) inconveniente

4. A) nueva
   B) tremenda
   C) segunda
   D) dos

5. A) de
   B) sobre
   C) en
   D) antes de

6. A) años
   B) días
   C) segundos
   D) lugares

7. A) hora
   B) madrugada
   C) tiempo
   D) reloj

Answers and Explanations to Practice Questions: Part B

Parecía que el pasado 6 de abril todo <u>estaba</u> listo para el despegue del transbordador Discovery cuya misión era la de realizar investigaciones atmosféricas y <u>estudios</u> solares, pero un <u>inconveniente</u> de última hora obligó a la Agencia Nacional de Aeronáutica y el Espacio (NASA) a abortar por <u>segunda</u> vez consecutiva el lanzamiento de la nave.

Al cierre de esta edición, la causa del incidente aún era desconocida y se esperaba que el viaje espacial pudiera concretarse <u>en</u> cualquier momento.

El apagado del motor ocurrió <u>segundos</u> antes de que los tres motores principales de la nave, alimentados por hidrógeno, fueran activados a las 2:32 de la <u>madrugada</u> del pasado 6 de abril, unos 6.6 segundos antes del lanzamiento.

Translation:

It seemed that last April 6 everything was ready to go for the launching of the shuttle Discovery, its mission to conduct atmospheric investigations and solar experiments, but a last minute difficulty forced the National Aeronautics and Space Administration (NASA) to abort for the second time the launching of the ship.

At the closing of this edition, the cause of the incident was unknown and it was expected that the space voyage could commence at any moment.

The shutdown of the motor came seconds before the three principal engines of the ship, run on hydrogen, were activated at 2:32 in the morning last April 6, some 6.6 seconds before the takeoff.

1. **A) was**
   B) will be
   C) would be
   D) is

The aborted launching of the shuttle already happened, so you need to use some kind of past tense. Since there is only one choice that's a past tense, you don't really need to think about which past tense applies. If you had trouble determining whether the event was in the past, present, or future, don't forget to look forward–the word **obligó** later in the sentence tells you that it's past. There are always clues in the passage that help you fill the blanks, but it's up to you to look for them.

2. A) classes
    B) studies
    C) stories
    D) lectures

The adjective **solares** that follows the blank is a big help on this question, because the expressions "solar classes," "solar stories," and "solar lectures" are all awkward in this context when compared with "solar studies."

3. A) affair
    B) witness
    C) picture
    D) difficulty

Abortar, which means the same thing in English as it does in Spanish (to abort), tells you that something went wrong with the launch, so you want a negative word for the blank. This only leaves you with choices A and D, and "affair" isn't so much negative as it is neutral (affairs can be either good or bad). However, "difficulty" can only be negative.

4. A) new
    B) tremendous
    C) second
    D) two

It's easiest to think of this blank as part of the larger phrase **abortar por . . . vez**. In this context, only **segunda** makes any sense in the blank.

5. A) of
    B) on
    C) at
    D) before

This question asks which preposition is correct before **cualquier momento**, and is probably much easier if you've seen the expression before (if you haven't, put it on your list). However, there are a couple of answers that can be canceled because their meanings are off (like A and B).

6. A) years
    B) days
    C) seconds

D) places

If you think about the situation described in the passage, and read ahead in the last paragraph, you realize that the period of time you're looking for is very brief. Also, there is a clue earlier in the passage that helps you out on this question. **De última hora**, which appears in the first sentence, means "at the last moment."

7. A) hour
    B) morning
    C) time
    D) clock

When you discuss the time in Spanish, you give the hour followed by an expression that tells you what part of the day you're talking about. These expressions are **de la noche** (at night)**, de la tarde** (in the afternoon)**, de la mañana** (in the morning), etc. There is another expression besides **de la mañana** that means the same thing, and that's **de la madrugada**. **Madrugada** is usually used for the very early morning, whereas **mañana** is used for any time before noon.

CHAPTER SIX

Reading Comprehension

Welcome to part C, Reading Comprehension. Reading Comprehension is the last question type you will see on the exam. It is also probably the most difficult to see improvement on in a short period of time. Despite this, there are two good reasons why you shouldn't worry. The first is that you can afford to leave some (or most) of the reading comprehension blank and still come away with a great score. The second is that by carefully choosing the right passage(s) to leave blank you can make the reading comprehension section of this test much easier for yourself than it otherwise might be. As usual (and for the last time), the first step is to acquaint yourself with the directions:

> <u>Directions:</u> Read the following passages carefully for comprehension. Each passage is followed by a number of questions or incomplete statements. Select the answer or completion that is best according to the passage and fill in the corresponding oval on the answer sheet.

The section will consist of approximately 28 questions in total, broken down into approximately six passages with three to five questions following each passage. The passages range in length from one short paragraph to six (or more) short paragraphs. The longer passages are usually followed by more questions. We'll get into how to choose which passages to do later, but for now realize that the length of the passage tells you nothing about its difficulty, so don't assume that the long passages are the hardest ones.

One of the nicest things about reading comprehension is (as we mentioned earlier) that you really don't need to do very much of it in order to get your desired score. In terms of the big picture, you should not rush through parts A and B in order to get to the reading. In fact, since the other three parts lend themselves to POE and guessing accurately, you should do the opposite. Take your time on the questions that are the most "technique-able" (parts A and B), and if this means leaving some of the reading blank, then that's just fine. It's not that the reading comprehension is impossible, it's just that it lends itself less to shortcuts and techniques.

HOW TO CRACK THE SECTION

The first and most important step in beating the reading comprehension is choosing which passage(s) to do and which passages to skip. Luckily, you've already had an introduction to this type of decision in part B of the exam. The idea is very similar: if the writing style is familiar (i.e., you can understand it without a major struggle) and there isn't too much tough vocabulary, then you're probably looking at a passage that you should do. This doesn't mean that you must know every single word in the passage. In fact, most passages will have some words (if only one or two) that you don't know. If you can understand the gist of what's going on in the overall passage, then you can answer the questions that follow.

HOW TO READ

Over the years, you've probably developed a reading style that includes a pace at which you're comfortable reading, a certain amount of attention to detail, etc. When you know that someone is going to ask you questions about what you've read, you usually change your reading style to match the situation. You read much more slowly, and you pay much more attention to detail than you would if you were reading, say, an article in a newspaper. The reason for this is simple: you assume that by reading more slowly and carefully you will better understand what you've read. Makes sense, right? Unfortunately, even though it seems logical, this approach can be disastrous when it comes to the reading comprehension section of the SAT.

What usually happens when you try to read ultraslowly and virtually memorize the passage is that you finish reading with no sense of what the overall passage is about. You may have picked up a few details, but who knows if those particular details will be asked of you? What eventually happens is on each question (or at least on most questions) you end up going back to the passage and rereading what you just read a minute ago. This approach is time-consuming and can be very frustrating. There is a better way.

Looking back at the passage in order to find the answer to a question is a very good idea. The problem is the initial time wasted in trying to memorize the passage in one reading. If you're going to refer back to the passage anyway, then what's the point? It doesn't make sense to read the passage slowly and carefully twice, especially if one of those two readings doesn't help you answer questions.

READING COMPREHENSION OR TREASURE HUNT?

We know that the instructions to the section ask you to read for comprehension, but we also know that those same instructions are written by the folks at ETS. Is this really about reading for comprehension, or is it about answering a few silly questions? Right, it's about answering a few silly questions. Treat the reading comprehension like a treasure hunt, where the answers to the individual questions are hidden somewhere in the passage and your job is to find them. Here's the best way to approach that task.

GET THE BIG PICTURE

You've already seen that it's a waste of time to try to memorize the passage in one reading. Instead of trying to memorize the entire thing, your first reading should be dedicated to finding the **topic** and the **structure** of the passage. This means that if you finish your initial read and you know what the overall passage is about, and you know the main point of each paragraph, you read the passage properly. Don't worry about facts or details (like names, dates, places, titles, etc.). Focus on what the whole passage is about, and, in a very general sense, what each paragraph is about. A good way to test whether you've done this well is to try and summarize the passage in a few words (no more than five or six), and summarize the content of each paragraph in even fewer words. If you can do both these things, you've definitely got a handle on the big picture, and that's going to be a big help in answering the questions.

There's no way we can tell you how long this initial reading should take, simply because everyone reads at a different pace to begin with. We can tell you that if you're stopping to try and decipher the meaning of every foreign word you come across, or if you're reading the same difficult sentence over and over again, you've missed the boat. Focus on ideas, not on particular words or facts.

The point of reading this way is not to enable you to answer all the questions without looking back (we wish it were that easy, too). The point is to give yourself a sense of where things are, so that when a question asks about a particular fact or detail, you may not know the answer but you <u>do</u> know where to look to find it.

Answering Questions

Although there are some questions that ask you about general things (main idea, what the passage is about, etc.), most of the questions ask you about more specific things that come from a particular place in the passage. These two types of questions should be dealt with separately.

GENERAL QUESTIONS

Once you've finished your first reading, you should go right to the questions to see if there are any general ones. Why? Because if you know the topic and structure of the passage, you can answer any general question without looking back to the passage. The general questions (when they appear) ask you for precisely what you just read for: general ideas. Here are some examples of general questions:

¿De qué se trata este artículo?
What is this passage about?

¿Quién narra este pasaje?
Who narrates this passage?

Very few of these appear on a given reading section, but when they do appear they are very easy. Make sure to do the general questions first if you choose a passage that contains any.

SPECIFIC QUESTIONS

The vast majority of reading comprehension questions require you to refer back to the passage to find the answer. This is why it's so important to get a sense of structure before you attempt to answer them. Otherwise you waste lots of time looking for the part of the passage the question came from. The approach to these questions is simple:

— read the question
— locate the source of the question by using guide words (we'll discuss guide words in a bit)
— read carefully the section of the passage where the question came from
— go to the answers and find the one that matches what you just read

HOW DO YOU KNOW WHERE TO LOOK?

Any specific question will have a word or words that tell you what the question is about. I call these guide words, because they essentially guide you to the place in the passage where the question originated. If you can determine the subject of the question, you should be able to tell (at least roughly) where it came from. Now all that's left is for you to read the source of the question carefully, and match it up with one of your answer choices.

POE and Avoiding Trap Answers

There will be times on the Reading Comprehension questions when the correct answer is so obvious that it practically jumps off the page at you. Some of the time, however, it probably won't be quite that easy. If you know how to work through the answer choices efficiently, and know how they might try to stump you, even the hardest questions can be tamed.

PROCESS OF ELIMINATION

One of the biggest problems students have with this section is that they don't like any of the answer choices to some questions. It's as if on some questions the test writers forgot to include the correct answer in the choices. The key to process of elimination on part C is that when you're stuck, you should forget about finding the right answer and concentrate on finding wrong answers. If you read all four choices and none of them looks good to you, don't panic. A couple of them probably look pretty bad to you, and those are just as helpful as answers that look good. Cancel the ones you know are wrong, and choose whatever's left.

We know this is a bitter pill to swallow, but the fact is that sometimes you'll end up choosing an answer that you don't like or even understand. That's fine though, because if you're sure that three of the answers are incorrect, then you must have confidence that the last one is the right one. Too often students shy away from answers they don't understand or don't like. Unfortunately, this section has little to do with what you like or understand. You're looking for the answer that will earn you a point, not the one you agree with.

TRAP ANSWERS

On **general questions**, the main thing to be on the lookout for is answers that are too specific. Unlike the answer to a specific question, the answer to a general question can't be located in one particular place in the passage. This makes sense because the answer to a general question should encompass the contents of the entire passage.

The test writers try to trip you up by providing answers that come from one part of the passage or another, but are not general enough to be correct. These answers tend to be very tempting, because they are in the passage that you just finished reading and you recognize them. If the answer to a general question is about a specific part of the passage, it's probably a trap.

On **specific questions**, the most important thing to remember is that the correct answer must come from the passage. We know this seems obvious, but one of ETS's favorite tricks on these questions is to provide answers that are reasonable, logical, and that jell with the contents of the passage, but are not <u>in</u> the passage. For this reason it's important that you stick to what you read when you refer to the passage. Don't think in terms of what the author might think or what you think. What's on the page in black and white is all you need to answer these questions.

Right answers to specific questions won't be exact quotes from the passage, but they'll be pretty darn close. They'll have the same exact meaning as the corresponding words in the passage, with maybe a couple of the words moved around or changed so that it looks a little different. In other words, the right answers are <u>close</u> paraphrases of the passage.

QUESTION ORDER

The specific questions are best done in the order that they appear (although you want to follow the golden rule of skipping any question that looks really difficult). This is because the order of the questions usually follows the progression of the passage—early questions come from the beginning of the passage, the subsequent questions come from the middle of the passage, etc. Something that you read in the early part of the passage can sometimes help on a later question.

As there is with part B of the exam, there is a tendency on part C to feel as if you're not done until you've answered every question that pertains to a certain passage. You're done whenever you want to be done. In other words, if you've done all the questions that you understand and can easily find the answers to, then move on to the next passage and see if you can find a couple of easy questions there. To a certain extent, reading comprehension will be as easy (or as difficult) as you want to make it.

TYPES OF PASSAGES

The main types of passages that appear are fiction, history, and current events (newspaper or magazine articles). Although subject matter has nothing to do with the difficulty of a passage, you may find that a certain passage, because it's about a familiar topic, has vocabulary that you understand. Don't take this on faith. Read a few sentences to make sure.

Reading Comprehension Summary

— Choose the order in which you want to do the passages. Read a couple of sentences to see if the writing style is easy to follow and the vocabulary is manageable. If so, go for it. If not, look ahead for something easier.

— Read the passage for topic and structure only. Don't read for detail, and don't try to memorize the entire thing. The first read is for you to get a sense of the subject and the overall structure—that's it.

— Go straight to the general questions. If you read correctly, you should be able to answer any general questions without looking back to the passage. Very few passages have general questions, so don't expect to find a lot.

— Now, do the specific questions in order. For these, you're going to let the guide words in the question tell you where to look in the passage. Then read the area that the question comes from slowly and carefully. Find an answer choice that basically says the same thing in slightly different language. These questions are about paraphrasing, not about comprehension.

— Avoid specific answers on general questions, and on specific questions avoid answers that are reasonable but aren't from the passage.

— Don't be afraid to leave blanks if there are questions that stump you. You're done with a passage whenever you've answered all the questions that you can answer. Instead of banging your head against a wall trying to do the last remaining question on a passage, go on to the next passage and find something easier.

Practice Questions

PART C

> Directions: Read the following passages carefully for comprehension. Each passage is followed by a number of questions or incomplete statements. Select the answer or completion that is best according to the passage and fill in the corresponding oval on the answer sheet.

España, con una superficie aproximada de dos veces la del estado de Wyoming y una población de una vez y media la de California, está situado en el sudoeste de Europa, separada de Francia por los montes pirineos y de África por el estrecho de Gibraltar. Su territorio está formado por la península ibérica, excepto Portugal, y los archipiélagos de las islas Baleares, en el mar mediterráneo, y de las islas Canarias, en el océano atlántico. Además ejerce su soberanía en dos ciudades de la costa de Marruecos, Ceuta y Melilla, y no la ejerce en un peñón, en su propia costa, el Peñón de Gibraltar, que es una posesión inglesa.

El español, aunque tiene muy poco que ver en muchos aspectos con los habitantes del norte y centro de Europa, es europeo y latino, por su historia y por su cultura. A pesar de todo, algunos dicen que

"África empieza en los Pirineos," y esto se debe a la influencia que tuvieron los casi ocho siglos de dominación árabe.

Para mucha gente, los españoles son personas pequeñas, morenas, que pasan la vida cantando y bailando flamenco, muy aficionados a las corridas de toros, que les gusta mucho perder el tiempo hablando de todo en las tertulias y en la sobremesa y que cuando están contentos, que es muy frecuente, dicen "olé." Esta idea es tan falsa como la que en España mucha gente también tiene de los americanos. El americano típico, para ellos, es el cowboy, el gangster o el artista de Hollywood. Sin embargo hay españoles en Estados Unidos que han visto, oído, cantado y bailado más flamenco aquí que en España, lo mismo que la mayoría de los americanos no tienen nada que ver ni con un cowboy, ni con un gangster ni con Hollywood.

1. El pasaje se trata de

   (A) la geografía de España y los españoles.
   (B) los cowboys americanos
   (C) la influencia de la dominacion árabe en España
   (D) la manera en cual los españoles verdaderamente víven.

2. La superficie de España es de un tamaño

   (A) dos veces el tamaño de los Estados Unidos
   (B) dos veces el tamaño del estado de Wyoming
   (C) una vez y media el tamaño de California
   (D) igual al tamaño del Peñón de Gibraltar

3. ¿Qué díce el autor sobre la historia y cultura del español?

   (A) Tienen mucho en común con la historia y la cultura del centro de europa.
   (B) Son adoptados de la cultura africana.
   (C) Tienen muchos aspectos de la cultura americana.
   (D) Son una combinación de influencias latinas y europeas.

4. ¿Cuál de los ideas siguientes tienen muchos americanos de los españoles?

   (A) Que los españoles típicos son gangsters.
   (B) Que las mujeres españolas estan enamoradas con los cowboys americanos.
   (C) Que todos pasan el día bailando y cantando flamenco.
   (D) Que quisieran vivir en Hollywood.

Los hispánicos que habitan en Estados Unidos pueden clasificarse en tres grandes grupos: él de origen mexicano, y con él la gran emigración de centroamericanos de los últimos años; él de los puertorriqueños; y él de los cubanos. La presencia de cada uno de estos grupos tiene una razón diferente y llega también en época distinta. Así mismo, aunque pueden encontrarse individuos de cada grupo en cualquier parte del país, cada uno de ellos está localizado en determinados lugares principalmente: los mexicanos y centroamericanos en el sudoeste y en la ciudad de Chicago, los puertorriqueños en Nueva York y los cubanos en la Florida. Considerados todos juntos como un grupo, tienen una gran importancia social, económica y política, pues aunque debido a la enorme emigración ilegal y constante no se conoce realmente su número, son muchos millones, y además tiene un índice de crecimiento mayor que el medio del país.

El principal problema que ha tenido y aún tiene este grupo, considerado en conjunto, es él de la discriminación de que es objeto por algunos sectores de la población del país, la cual ha disminuido mucho en años recientes gracias al interés del gobierno y algunos sectores de la población que quieren eliminar este problema definitivamente. Esta discriminación no es nada nuevo, ni exclusivo de este país ni de la población de origen anglosajón. Principalmente es un rechazo de una cultura por parte de otra, lo cual se agrava por el hecho de que conviven ambas en el mismo país. Tampoco es un problema exclusivo entre hispánicos y anglosajones, sino que lo han sufrido o lo sufren todavía muchos otros grupos, como los judíos, los italianos, y los negros. Y además, en muchos casos, o generalmente, el rechazo es mutuo, lo cual hace más difícil encontrar una solución.

5. ¿Dónde se puede encontrar la mayoría de los cubanos en los Estados Unidos?

(A) En Nueva York.
(B) En Chicago.
(C) En la Florida.
(D) En el sudoeste.

6. ¿Cuál es el problema que tienen los grupos hispánicos de quienes se trata el pasaje?

(A) La discriminación que exíste en este país.
(B) La dificultad de encontrar trabajo legítimo.
(C) La falta de colegios donde pueden aprender inglés.
(D) El gran índice de crecimiento que han realizado.

7. ¿Quién (o qué) tiene la culpa por la discriminación que existe?

(A) los anglosajones
(B) los judíos, los italianos, y los negros
(C) el gobierno de los Estados Unidos
(D) el rechazo mutuo entre culturas que tienen que vivir juntas

8. ¿Qué solución del problema de la discriminación se ofrece en el pasaje?

(A) Que las culturas diferentes se traten de entender una a la otra.
(B) Que todos los hispánicos regresen a sus países de origen.
(C) Solamente se dice que la solución no será fácil.
(D) Que el gobierno trate de pasar leyes que prohiben la discriminación.

Answers and Explanations to Reading Comprehension Questions

Here's a translation of the passage:

Spain, with a surface approximately two times that of the state of Wyoming, and a population one and a half times that of California, is located in the southwest of Europe, separated from France by the Pyrenees mountains and from Africa by the strait of Gibraltar. Its territory consists of the Iberian peninsula, except for Portugal, and the archipelagos of the Balearic Islands, in the Mediterranean Sea, and the Canary Islands, in the Atlantic Ocean. It also exercises its sovereignty over two cities on the coast of Morocco, Ceuta and Melilla, but does not exercise it over a rock, on its own coast, the Rock of Gibraltar, which is an English possession.

The Spaniard, although he has little to do in many ways with the inhabitants of northern and central Europe, is European and Latin, in his history and his culture. Nevertheless, some say that "Africa begins in the Pyrenees," and this is due to the influence of almost eight centuries of Arab domination.

For many, Spaniards are small, dark people who spend their lives singing and dancing flamenco, who are very fond of bullfights, who love to spend time talking at social gatherings or at the dinner table and when they're happy, which is rather often, say "ole." This idea is as false as the one that many people in Spain have of Americans. The typical American, for them, is the cowboy, the gangster, or the artist in Hollywood. However there are Spaniards in the United States that have seen, heard, sung, and danced more flamenco here than in Spain, just as the majority of Americans have nothing to do with cowboys, gangsters, or Hollywood.

1. The passage is about

   (A) the geography of Spain, and the Spanish
   (B) American cowboys
   (C) the influence of the Arab domination in Spain
   (D) the way in which the Spaniards truly live

This is a general question, so its answer won't be located in any one specific place in the passage. Instead, the answer is sort of a brief, general summary of the content of the three paragraphs.

2. The surface of Spain is of a size

   (A) twice the size of the United States
   (B) twice the size of the state of Wyoming
   (C) one and a half times the size of California
   (D) equal to the Rock of Gibraltar

The answer to this question is located in the beginning of the first paragraph. The lead word **superficie** is located only in that one area of the passage, and that's a big hint that that's where they took the question from.

3. What does the author say about the history and culture of the Spaniard?

   (A) They have much in common with the history and culture of central Europe.
   (B) They are borrowed from African culture.
   (C) They contain many aspects of American culture.
   (D) They are a combination of Latin and European influences.

The answer to this one is in the middle paragraph, which basically talks about the origins of the Spaniard. The guide words in the question are **historia y cultura**, which are found only in that middle paragraph.

4. Which of the following ideas do many people have about the Spanish?

   (A) That the typical Spaniards are gangsters.
   (B) That the Spanish women are in love with the American cowboy.
   (C) That they all spend the day dancing and singing flamenco.
   (D) That they'd like to live in Hollywood.

This question doesn't really have guide words, but since the entire third paragraph is about the mutual stereotypes that Americans and Spaniards subscribe to, it isn't too tough to locate the source of the question. You <u>do</u> have to read the question carefully, though, because some of the wrong answers are misconceptions Spaniards have about Americans and the question asks for the opposite.

Here's a translation of the passage:

The Hispanics that live in the United States can be classified in three large groups: those of Mexican origin, as well as the large immigration of Central Americans in recent years; Puerto Ricans; and Cubans. The presence of each one of these groups is for a different reason, and each arrived in a different era. Nevertheless, although you can find individuals from each group in any part of the country, each of the groups is principally located in particular areas: the Mexicans and Central Americans in the southwest and in the city of Chicago, the Puerto Ricans in New York and the Cubans in Florida. Considered all part of one big group, they have a great importance socially, economically and politically, and although due to the enormous illegal and continuing immigration their precise numbers aren't known, there are many millions, and furthermore their growth rate is larger than the U.S. average.

The principal problem that this group has had and continues to have, as a group, is that it is the object of discrimination of certain sectors of the population in this country, which has diminished much in recent years thanks to the interest of the government and of some sectors of the population who want to eliminate this problem definitively. This discrimination is nothing new, nor is it unique to this country or the people of Anglo-Saxon origin. Principally it is a rejection of one culture by another, which is aggravated by the fact that they live together in one country. It is not only a problem between Hispanics and Anglo-Saxons either, but something that has been suffered or is being suffered by many other groups, such as Jews, Italians, and African Americans. Furthermore, in many cases, or generally, the rejection is mutual, and this makes it even more difficult to find a solution.

5. Where can you find the majority of Cubans in the United States?

(A) in New York
(B) in Chicago
(C) in Florida
(D) in the Southwest

Dónde se puede encontrar is the "guide phrase" in this question, and it tells you to look in the first paragraph, around the middle.

6) What is the problem that the Hispanic groups mentioned in the passage have?

   (A) the discrimination that exists in this country
   (B) the difficulty in finding legitimate work
   (C) the lack of schools where they can learn English
   (D) the large growth rate that they've realized

This answer is located in the very beginning of the second paragraph, and your guide word is **problema**, which is mentioned in the very first sentence of that paragraph. This is a good example of a question where it is crucial that you not rely on intuition to choose answers to these questions. The only answer that is really bizarre is D, which is a "words out of context" trap answer. The other three things all <u>could</u> be problems that Hispanics in this country have, but only one of them is mentioned in the passage. You're not going to have to dig too much to find the answer to a question: it'll be a paraphrase of some part of the passage (with the exception of general questions). If something isn't mentioned in the passage, even if it makes sense to you, it's not going to be a correct answer.

7) Who (or what) is to blame for the discrimination that exists?

   (A) the Anglo-Saxons
   (B) the Jews, the Italians, and the African Americans
   (C) the United States government
   (D) the mutual rejection between cultures that have to live together

Once again, no real guide words in this question, but the answer must be somewhere in the second paragraph because that's where discrimination is discussed. The answer is towards the end of that paragraph.

8) What solution to the problem of discrimination is offered in the passage?

   (A) that the different cultures try to understand one another
   (B) that all the Hispanics return to their countries of origin
   (C) it only says that the solution won't be easy
   (D) that the government try to pass laws that prohibit discrimination

Although some (or all) of these answers may look attractive to you, once again it's what the <u>passage</u> says that we're concerned with. The answer lies at the end of the second paragraph.

CHAPTER SEVEN

The Princeton Review SAT II: Spanish Subject Test

SAT II: SPANISH SUBJECT TEST

SECTION 1

Your responses to the Spanish Subject Test questions must be filled in on Section One of your answer sheet (the box on the front of the answer sheet). Marks on any other section will not be counted toward your Spanish Subject Test score.

When your supervisor gives the signal, turn the page and begin the Spanish Subject Test. There are 100 numbered ovals on the answer sheet and 85 questions in the Spanish Subject Test. Therefore, use only ovals 1 to 85 for recording your answers.

PLEASE NOTE THAT YOUR ANSWER SHEET HAS FIVE ANSWER POSITIONS MARKED A, B, C, D, E, WHILE THE QUESTIONS THROUGHOUT THIS TEST CONTAIN ONLY FOUR CHOICES. BE SURE <u>NOT</u> TO MAKE ANY MARKS IN COLUMN E.

Part A

<u>Directions:</u> This part consists of a number of incomplete statements, each having four suggested completions. Select the most appropriate completion and fill in the corresponding oval on the answer sheet.

1. Si quieres ver el principio de la película, llega al teatro ...

   (A) más tarde
   (B) sin dinero
   (C) a tiempo
   (D) por la noche

2. Cuando vivía en Nueva York, _____ mucho tiempo escuchando conciertos y visitando los museos.

   (A) pasaba
   (B) pasé
   (C) he pasado
   (D) pasaré

3. Mi abuelo quiere vivir en un sitio bien tranquilo porque no le gusta el ruido. Por eso se ha mudado ...

   (A) a una calle muy ruidosa
   (B) fuera de la ciudad
   (C) al centro del mundo
   (D) sin querer

4. ¿_____ museo prefieres, él de ciencia o él de arte?

   (A) Cuál
   (B) Qué
   (C) Cuánto
   (D) Quién

5. Si no tienes hambre, no ...

   (A) hables
   (B) cantes
   (C) comas
   (D) abras

6. No le conozco muy bien, pero la gente dice que _____ un tipo muy sincero e inteligente.

   (A) estamos
   (B) son
   (C) está
   (D) es

7. Consuelo no pudo tomar la taza de café porque estaba ...

   (A) bastante seca
   (B) demasiado rica
   (C) muy caliente
   (D) falta de aceite

8. Vamos a tomar el viaje en dos días en vez de uno porque nuestro destino es muy _____ aquí.

   (A) cerca de
   (B) lejos de
   (C) junto a
   (D) en frente de

GO ON TO THE NEXT PAGE →

9. Mi hermano nació tres años antes que yo; por eso es ...

 (A) más viejo
 (B) más alto
 (C) mi hermano favorito
 (D) muy pesado

10. ¿Si no te gusta la ley, por qué _____ los cuatro últimos años trabajando como abogado?

 (A) pasas
 (B) has pasado
 (C) pasarías
 (D) hemos pasado

11. En la biblioteca se encuentran ...

 (A) plumas
 (B) esperanzas
 (C) preguntas
 (D) libros

12. La bandera que vuela sobre el estadio es _____.

 (A) lo nuestro
 (B) las nuestras
 (C) la nuestra
 (D) lo mío

13. La sopa caliente me dió un dolor de dientes. Necesito ...

 (A) una silla
 (B) una muela
 (C) un dentista
 (D) un tornillo

14. Si tuviera la oportunidad deconocer al presidente, le _____ miles de sugerencias.

 (A) he dado
 (B) daba
 (C) daría
 (D) daré

15. Para ir a México el ... más rapido es éste.

 (A) camino
 (B) cielo
 (C) paseo
 (D) suelo

16. Ayer tuve mucho dolor en la espalda, pero hoy no _____ ninguno.

 (A) tienen
 (B) tenemos
 (C) tiene
 (D) tengo

17. El hermano de mi padre es el padre de mi ...

 (A) nieta
 (B) primo
 (C) abuelo
 (D) tía

18. García es nuestro cliente más estimado; siempre _____ damos lo que quiere.

 (A) la
 (B) le
 (C) él
 (D) les

19. Alberto se sienta y pide arroz con pollo y un vaso de vino. El está en ...

 (A) un restaurante
 (B) un circo
 (C) un banco
 (D) una zapatería

20. ¿_____cuándo empezaron a estudiar la historia española?

 (A) Hasta
 (B) Durante
 (C) Desde
 (D) En

GO ON TO THE NEXT PAGE

21. En abril las flores crecen rapidamente porque ...
bastante.

    (A) duran
    (B) llora
    (C) llueve
    (D) llega

22. Mi tío sabe cocinar los frijoles negros bastante
    _____.

    (A) bien
    (B) bueno
    (C) buenos
    (D) baños

23. El concierto que vimos anoche fue estupendo.
    ¡Esa ... de verdad sabe tocar!

    (A) partida
    (B) novela
    (C) comida
    (D) orquesta

24. Tengo miedo que la tormenta _____ durante la
    boda que vamos a tener en el patio.

    (A) llegue
    (B) llega
    (C) llegaría
    (D) llegará

25. Carlos es un muchacho muy pesado que siempre
    está metido en algún lío. No es milagro que todo el
    mundo lo ...

    (A) quiere
    (B) rechaza
    (C) ayuda
    (D) conoce

26. Yo manejé por dos horas para encontrar esa
    medicina— si no te _____ tomas te mato!

    (A) lo
    (B) le
    (C) las
    (D) la

27. Despues de dos años de investigaciones, el médico
    en fin ... una cura para la enfermedad.

    (A) descubrió
    (B) dirigió
    (C) abrió
    (D) buscó

28. Jamás hemos bailado la samba, pero si _____
    como bailar a lambada.

    (A) conocemos
    (B) conozco
    (C) saben
    (D) sabemos

29. Dicen que José Martí, el famoso autor cubano,
    empezó a escribir ... cuando tenía solamente seis
    años.

    (A) lápices
    (B) alfabetos
    (C) idiomas
    (D) poemas

GO ON TO THE NEXT PAGE

THERE ARE NO TEST MATERIALS ON THIS PAGE

GO ON TO THE NEXT PAGE

Part B

<u>Directions:</u> Each of the following passages contains numbered blanks indicating that words or phrases have been omitted from the text. First, read quickly thorugh the entire passage to determine its general meaning. Then read it a second time. For each numbered blank, choose the completion that is most appropriate given the context of the entire passage and fill in the corresponding oval on the answer sheet.

Emma dejó caer el papel. Su primera __(30)__ fue de malestar en el vientre y en las rodillas; luego de ciega culpa, de irrealidad, de frío, de __(31)__ ; luego, quiso ya __(32)__ en el día siguiente. Acto continuo comprendió que esa voluntad era inútil porque __(33)__ muerte de su padre era lo único que __(34)__ en el mundo, y __(35)__ sucediendo sin fin. Recogió el papel y se fue a su cuarto. Furtivamente lo __(36)__ en un cajón, como si de algún modo ya __(37)__ los hechos ulteriores.

30. (A) tiempo
    (B) vista
    (C) puesto
    (D) impresión

31. (A) juventud
    (B) temor
    (C) alegría
    (D) hambre

32. (A) estar
    (B) ser
    (C) estaré
    (D) ir

33. (A) lo
    (B) el
    (C) la
    (D) las

34. (A) entraba
    (B) crecía
    (C) había terminado
    (D) había sucedido

35. (A) seguiría
    (B) pararía
    (C) cambiaría
    (D) sentiría

36. (A) sacó
    (B) guardó
    (C) encontró
    (D) quitó

37. (A) sabe
    (B) dudaba
    (C) conociera
    (D) empezó

Después __(38)__ haber mandado dos expediciones a explorar la costa de México, el gobernador de Cuba __(39)__ otra expedición bajo el mando de Hernán Cortés en 1519. En las tres expediciones __(40)__ parte un soldado que se __(41)__ Bernal Díaz del Castillo. __(42)__ soldado, cuando ya era casi viejo y __(43)__ retirado en Guatemala, __(44)__ sus recuerdos de las guerras mexicanas, que forman la mejor narración __(45)__ la conquista de México y que se titula "Historia verdadera de la conquista de la nueva España."

La expedición de Cortés constaba de once navíos que __(46)__ poco más de seiscientos hombres y dieciséis __(47)__ Cuando estaba listo Cortés __(48)__ salir, el gobernador trató de quitarle el mando, pero él decidió hacerse a la mar.

38. (A) que
    (B) de
    (C) a
    (D) por

39. (A) le puso fin a
    (B) ensayó
    (C) preguntó
    (D) organizó

40. (A) hizo
    (B) dio
    (C) dejó
    (D) tomó

GO ON TO THE NEXT PAGE

41. (A) llamó
    (B) llama
    (C) llamaba
    (D) había llamado

42. (A) Este
    (B) Esa
    (C) Un
    (D) Lo

43. (A) paraba
    (B) pensaba
    (C) oía
    (D) vivía

44. (A) escribió
    (B) corrió
    (C) perdió
    (D) pidió

45. (A) encima de
    (B) junto a
    (C) sobre
    (D) en vez de

46. (A) llevaba
    (B) llevaron
    (C) llevaban
    (D) llevan

47. (A) automóviles
    (B) aviones
    (C) caballos
    (D) guantes

48. (A) por
    (B) para
    (C) en
    (D) de

Pero hoy, esta mañana fría, en que tenemos más prisa que nunca, la niña y yo _(49)_ de largo delante de la fila tentadora de autos parados. Por _(50)_ vez en la vida vamos al colegio . . . Al colegio, le digo, no _(51)_ ir en taxi. Hay que correr un poco por las calles, hay que tomar el metro, hay que _(52)_ luego, en un sitio determinado, a un autobús . . . Es que yo he escogido un colegio muy _(53)_ para mi niña, ésa es la verdad; un colegio que _(54)_ mucho, pero está muy lejos . . . Sin embargo, yo no estoy impaciente hoy, ni _(55)_ , y la niña lo sabe. Es ella

ahora la que inicia una caricia tímida con su manita _(56)_ la mía; y por primera vez me doy cuenta de que su mano de cuatro años es _(57)_ mi mano grande: tan decidida, tan poco suave, tan nerviosa como la mía.

49. (A) pasamos
    (B) entramos
    (C) dabamos
    (D) pagamos

50. (A) ninguna
    (B) primera
    (C) siempre
    (D) costumbre

51. (A) se engaña
    (B) conocemos
    (C) se puede
    (D) sobran

52. (A) dormir
    (B) tocar
    (C) jugar
    (D) caminar

53. (A) cerrado
    (B) lejano
    (C) oscuro
    (D) dificil

54. (A) me gusta
    (B) odio
    (C) no conozco
    (D) dudamos

55. (A) vieja
    (B) alta
    (C) cansada
    (D) fresca

56. (A) dentro de
    (B) fuera de
    (C) cerca de
    (D) sin

57. (A) diferente a
    (B) igual a
    (C) cerca de
    (D) encima de

GO ON TO THE NEXT PAGE

Part C

Directions: Read the following passages carefully for comprehension. Each passage is followed by a number of questions or incomplete statements. Select the answer or completion that is best according to the passage and fill in the corresponding oval on the answer sheet.

Al pasar ante una granja, un perro mordió a mi amigo. Entramos a ver al granjero y le preguntamos si era suyo el perro. El granjero, para evitarse complicaciones, dijo que no era suyo.

— Entonces—dijo mi amigo– présteme una hoz para cortarle la cabeza, pues debo llevarla al Instituto para que la analicen.

En aquel momento apareció la hija del granjero y pidió a su padre que no permitiera que le cortáramos la cabeza al perro.

— Si es suyo el perro—dijo mi amigo,— enséñeme el certificado de vacunación antirrábica.

El hombre entró en la granja, y tardó largo rato en salir. Mientras tanto, el perro se acercó y mi amigo dijo:

— No me gusta el aspecto de este animal.

En efecto, babeaba y los ojos parecían arderle en las órbitas. Incluso andaba dificultosamente.

— Hace unos días– dijo la jóven—le atropelló una bicicleta.

El granjero nos dijo que no encontraba el certificado de vacunación.

— Debo haberlo perdido.

— La vida de un hombre puede estar en juego— intervine yo– Díganos, con toda sinceridad, si el perro está vacunado o no.

El hombre bajó la cabeza y murmuró:

— Está sano.

58. ¿Qué les pasó a los tipos cuando pasaron por la granja?

(A) a uno de ellos le mordió un perro
(B) un granjero les pidió direcciones
(C) empezó a llover
(D) perdieron su perro

59. ¿Por qué el granjero les dijo que el perro no era suyo?

(A) no sabía de quien era el perro
(B) no conocía los tipos que vinieron a la puerta
(C) no quería tomar culpa por lo que había hecho el perro
(D) no le gustaban los perros

60. ¿Qué le pidió su hija al granjero?

(A) que le diera dinero para comprar caramelos
(B) que llevara el perro al médico
(C) que le diera comida al perro
(D) que no permitiera que los hombres dañaran al perro

61. ¿Qué le pidieron los tipos al granjero?

(A) un vaso de agua
(B) el certificado de vacunación rábica
(C) un teléfono para llamar a la policía
(D) prueba que verdaderamente era granjero

62. ¿Como parecia el perro del granjero?

(A) sano y de buen humor
(B) enfermo, como si tuviese rabias
(C) joven y lleno de energia
(D) serio y pensativo

63. ¿Qué razón dio la niña por la manera en cual el perro se portaba?

(A) tuvo un accidente con una bicicleta
(B) no le gusta la gente
(C) es un perro muy feróz
(D) tuvo mucha hambre

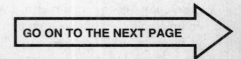

GO ON TO THE NEXT PAGE

64. ¿En fin, que les dice el granjero a los tipos?

(A) que deben ir al hospital
(B) que deben adaptar un perro
(C) que se vayan de la granja ahora mismo
(D) que el perro no tiene ninguna enfermedad

En nuestra oficina regía el mismo presupuesto desde el año mil novecientos veintitantos, o sea desde una época en que la mayoría de nosotros estábamos luchando con la geografía y con los quebrados. Sin embargo, el Jefe se acordaba del acontecimiento y a veces, cuando el trabajo disminuía, se sentaba familiarmente sobre uno de nuestros escritorios, y así, con las piernas colgantes que mostraban después del pantalón unos inmaculados calcetines blancos, nos relataba con su vieja emoción y las quinientas noventa y ocho palabras de costumbre, el lejano y magnífico día en que su Jefe—él era entonces Oficial Primero– le había palmeado el hombro y le había dicho: "Muchacho, tenemos presupuesto nuevo," con la sonrisa amplia y satisfecha del que ya ha calculado cuantas camisas podrá comprar con el aumento.

65. ¿Por más o menos cuánto tiempo han tenido el mismo presupuesto?

(A) por varias decadas
(B) por varios siglos
(C) por unas cuantas semanas
(D) desde ayer

66. El Jefe hacía el cuento cuando

(A) estaba triste
(B) había tomado demasiado cerveza
(C) el trabajo era menos de lo corriente
(D) tenían una fiesta

67. El cuento del presupuesto nuevo que hacía el Jefe

(A) tenía calcetines blancos
(B) siempre era diferente
(C) era interesante
(D) siempre era el mismo

68. ¿Cuál era la reacción del Jefe cuando su jefe le contó del presupuesto nuevo?

(A) se fue de la compañía
(B) se puso muy contento
(C) le dió un abrazo a su jefe
(D) compró camisas nuevas

Para los arqueólogos y los historiadores, la civilización maya es, sin duda alguna, la que alcanzó un mayor nivel de desarrollo entre todas las civilizaciones que existían antes de la llegada de Colón. Aunque todavía hay muchos secretos que no se han descifrado con relación a los mayas, parece que esta civilización empezó varios siglos antes del nacimiento de Cristo. Sin embargo se sabe que los mayas abandonaron los grandes centros ceremoniales en el siglo X de nuestra era.

Los primeros templos que construyeron son de forma de pirámide de cuatro lados con una gran escalinata. Sobre la pirámide hay un edificio de un piso normalmente y en algunos casos de dos, y en ellos podemos ver relieves de arcilla y esculturas de madera y piedra caliza. Las figuras son siempre de perfil y en ellas se puede apreciar los adornos y joyas que usaban. En la clasificación que se ha hecho de las épocas de esta civilización, se llama preclásica a la época primera, que se desarrolla en Guatemala y Honduras, y que segun los arqueólogos duró hasta el fin del siglo III de nuestra era.

69. ¿Qué piensan los arqueólogos y los historiadores de la civilización maya?

(A) que era una civilización muy avanzada
(B) que los mayas escribieron libros magníficos
(C) que conocieron a Colón
(D) que tenían muchos secretos

70. ¿Cuándo empezó la civilización maya?

(A) en el siglo X de nuestra era
(B) inmediatamente antes de la llegada de Colón
(C) varios siglos antes del nacimiento de Cristo
(D) varios siglos después del nacimiento de Cristo

71. ¿Cómo parecían los primeros templos de los mayas?

(A) fueron edificios muy bajos
(B) fueron hechos de madera y piedra caliza
(C) fueron pirámides de cuatro lados
(D) fueron casas corrientes, como las que tenemos hoy

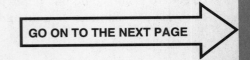
GO ON TO THE NEXT PAGE

72. ¿Qué se puede decir de las esculturas que hicieron los mayas?

    (A) tenían escalinatas grandes
    (B) dan información sobre las joyas y adornos que usaban
    (C) cuesta mucho comprarlas
    (D) se pueden encontrar en los museos famosos

73. ¿Dónde empezó y se desarrolló la época preclásica?

    (A) en Nicaragua
    (B) en México
    (C) en la época preclásica
    (D) en Honduras y Guatemala

74. El pasaje se trata de

    (A) la civilizacion y architectura maya.
    (B) la influencia de Cristo sobre la civilizacion maya.
    (C) las diferencias entre nuestra civilizacion y la de los maya.
    (D) los adornos y las joyas que usaban los mayas.

Dentro de pocos años se cumplirán cinco siglos ya del encuentro de Europa con América. Fue poco después de la medianoche del 11 al 12 de octubre de 1492, cuando Rodrigo de Triana, un tripulante de la carabela "La Niña," la cual se había adelantado a "La Santa María," donde iba Colón, dio el grito de "Tierra, tierra." El lugar era muy cercano a la Florida, una pequeña isla llamada Guanahani a la que Colón llamó San Salvador y que pertenece al archipiélago de las Lucayas o Bahamas.

Lo que Colón encontró y describe en sus cartas a los Reyes Católicos fue mucha pobreza y gente que iba desnuda, como su madre los parió, todos jóvenes, con hermosos cuerpos, cabellos gruesos como los caballos y cortos que les caen por encima de las cejas y otros largos por detrás.

Pocos días después, descubrió la costa de Cuba, a la que llamó Juana, por la hija de los reyes. Por entonces, Martín Alonzo Pinzón, que mandaba "La Pinta," se separó de la expedición, lo cual consideró Colón como una deserción, aunque disimuló por mantener la unidad de la expedición.

Al cabo de unos días llegó a Haití, a la cual llamó La Española, pero por los muchos bajos y arrecifes que había, "La Santa María" encalló.

75. ¿Quién fue el primero que vió tierra en la expedición?

    (A) un tripulante que se llamaba Rodrigo de Triana
    (B) Colón
    (C) La Niña
    (D) Guanahani, el mejor amigo de Colón

76. ¿Cómo era la gente que Colón encontró?

    (A) muy pobres, pero también hermosos
    (B) violentes y agresivos
    (C) más inteligente que los tripulantes
    (D) muy miedosos y confundidos

77. ¿Qué descubrió Colón unos días después que descubrió a San Salvador?

    (A) el archipiélago de las Bahamas
    (B) la isla que hoy se llama Cuba
    (C) Haití
    (D) cabellos gruesos

78. ¿Cuál fue la reacción de Colón cuando Martín Alonzo Pinzón se separó de la expedición?

    (A) se puso furioso
    (B) empezó a llorar
    (C) dio la impresión que no supo lo que había pasado
    (D) mandó otra carabela tras de él

79. ¿Cómo terminó en fin La Santa María?

    (A) regresó a Espana
    (B) se perdió y nunca lo han encontrado
    (C) fue hundido
    (D) encalló como resultado de los arrecifes y bajos

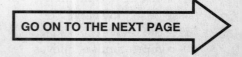
GO ON TO THE NEXT PAGE

Si no fuera por el gusto exigente de los bebedores de café de Arabia Saudita, el pueblo guatemalteco de Cobán, al otro lado del mundo, estaría en problemas.

Cobán, capital de la región montañosa de Alta Verapaz en Guatemala, es la fuente de la mayor parte del cardamomo que consume el mundo árabe: una especia dulce, picante y sumamente aromática que se emplea en la cocina de la India. De hecho, el café de cardamomo, conocido en el mundo árabe como *kahwe hal*, es considerado un símbolo de hospitalidad en todo el Cercano Oriente.

En Cobán, famoso por su iglesia católica del siglo XVI y las ruinas mayas que se encuentran en los alrededores, prácticamente nadie habla árabe y ninguno de sus 125,000 habitantes pone cardamomo en el café. Sin embargo, todos conecen perfectamente la conexión que existe entre la especia y el mundo árabe. "El cardamomo es la base de nuestra economía, y Guatemala es el principal exportador del mundo."

80. ¿En que país en particular toman el café de cardamomo?

   (A) en Guatemala
   (B) en Arabia Saudita
   (C) en la Alta Verapaz
   (D) en el Cercano Oriente

81. ¿Qué es el cardamomo?

   (A) un tipo de café raro
   (B) una especia
   (C) un estilo de cocinar indio
   (D) un tipo de árbol

82. ¿Como sabe el cardamomo?

   (A) picante, pero también dulce
   (B) un poco amargo
   (C) casi no tiene sabor
   (D) sabe como el café clombiano

83. ¿Por qué es conocido la ciudad de Cobán?

   (A) por el cardamomo
   (B) por el mejor café en el Norte América
   (C) por sus ruinas, y por su iglesia del siglo XVI
   (D) por la comida india

84. ¿Cuál es la conexión entre el mundo árabe y Guatemala?

   (A) en Guatemala todos hablan árabe
   (B) en los dos lugares les encanta el café de cardamomo
   (C) Guatemala exporta mucho de la especia al mundo árabe
   (D) de verdad no hay conexión entre los dos lugares

85. ¿Cuál sería un buen título para el pasaje?

   (A) "Cobán: la ciudad en las montañas"
   (B) "La economía de Guatemala"
   (C) "Los cafés del mundo"
   (D) "Cardamomo: lo que junta Guatemala con el mundo árabe"

STOP

How to Score the Spanish Subject Test

When you take the real exam, they (the proctors) take away your exam and your bubble sheet and send it to New Jersey where a computer looks at the pattern of filled-in ovals on your exam and gives you a score. We couldn't include a computer with this book, so we are providing this more primitive way of scoring your exam.

DETERMINING YOUR SCORE

STEP 1 Using the answers on the next page, determine how many questions you got right and how many you got wrong on the test. Remember, questions that you do not answer do not count as either right answers or wrong answers.

STEP 2 List the number of right answers here.   (A) _____

STEP 3* List the number of wrong answers here.
Now divide that number by 3. (Use a calculator if you're feeling particularly lazy.)   (B)_____ ÷ 3 = _____

STEP 4 Subtract the number of wrong answers divided by 3 from the number of correct answers. Round this score to the nearest whole number. This is your raw score.
         (A) − (B) =   _____

STEP 5 To determine your real score, take the number from Step 4 above and look it up in the left column of the Score Conversion Table on page 231; the corresponding score on the right is your score on the exam.

---

*In doing step 3, some rather timid students notice that they lose a fraction of a point if they put down a wrong answer. These timid students get the idea that maybe guessing isn't such a good idea. These students are wrong. Guess whenever you can eliminate anything.

Answers to the Princeton Review
Spanish Subject Test

Question Number	Correct Answer	Right	Wrong	Question Number	Correct Answer	Right	Wrong	Question Number	Correct Answer	Right	Wrong
1	C	___	___	30	D	___	___	59	C	___	___
2	A	___	___	31	B	___	___	60	D	___	___
3	B	___	___	32	D	___	___	61	B	___	___
4	A	___	___	33	C	___	___	62	B	___	___
5	C	___	___	34	D	___	___	63	A	___	___
6	D	___	___	35	A	___	___	64	D	___	___
7	C	___	___	36	B	___	___	65	A	___	___
8	B	___	___	37	C	___	___	66	C	___	___
9	A	___	___	38	B	___	___	67	D	___	___
10	B	___	___	39	D	___	___	68	B	___	___
11	D	___	___	40	D	___	___	69	A	___	___
12	C	___	___	41	C	___	___	70	C	___	___
13	C	___	___	42	A	___	___	71	C	___	___
14	C	___	___	43	D	___	___	72	B	___	___
15	A	___	___	44	A	___	___	73	D	___	___
16	D	___	___	45	C	___	___	74	A	___	___
17	B	___	___	46	C	___	___	75	A	___	___
18	B	___	___	47	C	___	___	76	A	___	___
19	A	___	___	48	B	___	___	77	B	___	___
20	C	___	___	49	A	___	___	78	C	___	___
21	C	___	___	50	B	___	___	79	D	___	___
22	A	___	___	51	C	___	___	80	B	___	___
23	D	___	___	52	D	___	___	81	B	___	___
24	A	___	___	53	B	___	___	82	A	___	___
25	B	___	___	54	A	___	___	83	C	___	___
26	D	___	___	55	C	___	___	84	C	___	___
27	A	___	___	56	A	___	___	85	D	___	___
28	D	___	___	57	B	___	___				
29	D	___	___	58	A	___	___				

	THE PRINCETON REVIEW SPANISH SUBJECT TEST SCORE CONVERSION TABLE				
Raw Score	Scaled Score	Raw Score	Scaled Score	Raw Score	Scaled Score
85	750	45	540	5	370
84	740	44	540	4	370
83	730	43	530	3	360
82	730	42	530	2	360
81	720	41	520	1	350
80	720	40	520	0	340
79	710	39	510	−1	340
78	710	38	510	−2	330
77	700	37	500	−3	330
76	700	36	500	−4	320
75	690	35	490	−5	320
74	690	34	490	−6	310
73	680	33	480	−7	310
72	680	32	480	−8	300
71	670	31	470	−9	300
70	670	30	470	−10	300
69	660	29	470	−11	290
68	660	28	460	−12	290
67	650	27	460	−13	280
66	650	26	450	−14	280
65	640	25	450	−15	270
64	640	24	450	−16	270
63	630	23	440	−17	260
62	630	22	440	−18	260
61	620	21	430	−19	250
60	620	20	430	−20	250
59	610	19	430	−21	240
58	610	18	420	−22	240
57	600	17	420	−23	240
56	600	16	420	−24	230
55	590	15	410	−25	230
54	590	14	410	−26	220
53	590	13	410	−27	220
52	580	12	400	−28	210
51	570	11	400	−29	210
50	570	10	400		
49	560	9	390		
48	560	8	390		
47	550	7	380		
46	550	6	380		

CHAPTER EIGHT

SAT II: Spanish Subject Test Explanations

Part A

1. If you want to see the beginning of the film, arrive at the theater ...

   (A) later
   (B) without money
   (C) on time
   (D) at night

The key phrase in this sentence is **si quieres ver el principio**. If you were able to get this much, you could determine that time had something to do with the answer, and that would eliminate B and D. What would make more sense in terms of seeing the beginning of something: arriving later, or arriving on time? On time makes more sense, and C is the correct answer.

2. When I lived in New York I _____ a lot of time hearing concerts and visiting the museums.

    (A) used to pass
    (B) passed
    (C) have passed
    (D) will pass

Since the sentence refers to the past, the answer must be some kind of past tense and since **pasaré** is the future you can immediately scratch D. The other three choices are all past tenses, but since the action described is no longer happening (**vivía** implies that you no longer live there), and it occurred over a period of time in the past, the imperfect is the tense you're looking for.

3. My grandfather wants to live in a peaceful place because he doesn't like noise. That's why he's moved ...

    (A) to a noisy street
    (B) outside of the city
    (C) to the center of the Earth
    (D) by mistake

If you understood either the part about not liking noise or the part about wanting to live peacefully you could eliminate A. Choices C and D are sort of ridiculous, and so B is your best bet (and the correct answer).

4. _____ museum do you prefer, the science museum or the art museum?

    (A) Which
    (B) What
    (C) How much
    (D) Who

Quién is used to refer to people, and since we're talking about museums you can eliminate D. **Cuánto** is used to inquire about quantities, so we're down to A and B. **Qué** is often used in questions ("Qué hora es?"), but since a choice is asked for, **cuál** is used instead of **qué**.

5. If you're not hungry, then don't ...

    (A) talk
    (B) sing
    (C) eat
    (D) open

The only answer that is even remotely related to food here is C, and that is the correct answer.

6. I don't know him well, but people say that he
_____ a sincere and intelligent guy.

(A) are
(B) are
(C) is
(D) is

If you know when to use **ser** and when to use **estar**, this question is a piece of cake. Since we're talking about one person (**le** is a singular pronoun) A and B can be easily eliminated. Now for the subtle part. Does the sentence give us any reason to suspect that this person's admirable qualities are going to change or disappear in the near future? No, therefore **ser** is correct.

7. Consuelo couldn't drink the cup of coffee because it was ...

(A) dry enough
(B) too tasty
(C) very hot
(D) lacking oil

This one is a bit tricky, but if you understood the first part of the sentence the question is definitely doable (probably a second-pass question). What would keep someone from drinking something? The only choice that makes any sense is C.

8. We're going to make the trip in two days instead of one because our destination is _____ here.

(A) near to
(B) far from
(C) next to
(D) in front of

The meaning of this sentence gives some helpful clues. In fact, since the duration of the trip is going to be twice what was expected, the only answer that makes any sense is **lejos de**.

9. My brother was born three years before I was; that's why he's ...

(A) older
(B) taller
(C) my favorite brother
(D) very annoying

Although each of the answers is something a brother could be, "born three years before" points strongly to choice A, which is correct.

10. If you don't like the law, why _____ the past
    four years working as a lawyer?

    (A) do you spend
    (B) have you spent
    (C) would you spend
    (D) have we spent

"The past four years" tells you that we need some type of past tense, so cancel A and C. We know that these answers sound good both in Spanish and in English, but that's precisely why your ear is only used as a last resort for guessing. Exhaust what you know first, then use your ear if it's all you've got left to go on. Since we're not sure whether this person is a lawyer now or will continue to be one, the present perfect is called for.

11. In the library you find ...

    (A) pens
    (B) hopes
    (C) questions
    (D) books

This is a very straightforward question, that is, if you know the word for library. The corrrect answer is D. Be careful not to confuse **biblioteca** with **librería**, which means bookstore.

12. The flag that flies over the stadium is _____

    (A) ours (masculine)
    (B) ours (plural)
    (C) ours (fem. sing.)
    (D) mine (masculine)

The wrong answers here (as they do on many SST questions) are wrong because they don't agree with what they're replacing either in gender or in number. Since **la bandera** is singular and feminine, **la** is the correct pronoun.

13. The hot soup gave me a toothache. I need ...

    (A) a chair
    (B) a molar
    (C) a dentist
    (D) a screw

Toothache is the key word in this example. If you understood that much, you could easily have guessed C, which is correct.

14. If I were to have the chance to meet the president,
     I _____ him thousands of suggestions.

     (A) have given
     (B) gave
     (C) would give
     (D) will give

Si is your big clue that the conditional is used. The only choice that's in the conditional is C.

15. To go to Mexico, the fastest ... is this one.

     (A) road
     (B) sky
     (C) stroll
     (D) ground

Only one of the answers is something that would be involved in going to Mexico, and that answer is A. *Stroll* is a tricky choice because it sort of goes with *fastest*, but it makes no sense with the first part of the sentence.

16. Yesterday I had a lot of pain in my back, but today
     I don't _____ any.

     (A) have (ellos)
     (B) have (nosotros)
     (C) has
     (D) have (yo)

Somewhere on your exam you will probably see a question whose answer is the plain present tense, like this one. All four answers are in the present, so you have to pay special attention to the subject (**yo**).

17. My father's brother is the father of my ...

     (A) grandaughter
     (B) cousin
     (C) grandfather
     (D) aunt

This is a very tough question if you don't know most of the vocabulary. Your father's brother would be your uncle, who would be the father of your cousin, so B is correct. You could eliminate A, C, and D if you could determine that the answer would be someone in your generation, but even then the vocabulary is crucial on this particular question.

18. García is our most respected client—we always give _____ what he wants.

    (A) it (feminine)
    (B) (to) him
    (C) he
    (D) (to) them

Direct object or indirect object, that is the question. Since things are given <u>to</u> people, you have to use the type of pronoun that goes with prepositions, i.e., indirect.

19. Alberto sits down and requests chicken with rice and a glass of wine. He is in ...

    (A) a restaurant
    (B) a circus
    (C) a bank
    (D) a shoe store

If you caught any of the food words in this sentence you would guess A. None of the others is even in the ballpark.

20. _____ when did you begin studying Spanish history?

    (A) Until
    (B) During
    (C) Since
    (D) In

This is another preposition question, and once again meaning is your savior. The only choice that really works in terms of meaning is **desde**. **Durante cuándo** is redundant (you would just say **cuándo**), and **hasta cuándo** suggests that the speaker already knew you were studying Spanish history. However, the sentence suggests that he didn't.

21. In April the flowers grow quickly because it ... plenty

    (A) lasts
    (B) cries
    (C) rains
    (D) arrives

The trick here is that the answers are so similar sounding. What would make flowers grow quickly? *Rain*, so C is the best answer. *April* might have given you a hint (you know, April showers . . .).

22. My uncle knows how to make black beans pretty
    _____.

    (A) well
    (B) good (singular)
    (C) good (plural)
    (D) baths

Just thought we'd sneak an adjective vs. adverb question in for fun. **Bueno** (good) is an adjective, and since you are describing an action (how the black beans are made) an adverb is used. **Baños** is thrown in there to see if you're awake. It sort of sounds and looks like **buenos**.

23. The concert that we saw last night was excellent.
    That ... really knows how to play.

    (A) game
    (B) novel
    (C) meal
    (D) orchestra

The word *concert* points to D, which is the correct choice.

24. I'm afraid that the storm _____ during the wed-
    ding that we're going to have in the patio.

    (A) will arrive
    (B) arrives
    (C) would arrive
    (D) arrived

Expressions of fear are dead giveaways that you need to use the subjunctive. Then all you have to do is check the tense of the expression to tell you which subjunctive to use. **Tengo miedo** is in the present, so this time it's present subjunctive.

25. Carlos is an annoying kid who is always in some
    kind of trouble. That's why everyone ...

    (A) likes him
    (B) rejects him
    (C) helps him
    (D) knows him

There is some tough vocabulary here. Fortunately, there are lots of different clues that tell you that Carlos isn't a particularly likable fellow, and that makes B the best answer.

26. I drove for two hours looking for that medicine—
    if you don't take _____ I'll kill you!

    (A) it (masculine)
    (B) (to) him
    (C) them (feminine)
    (D) it (feminine)

The pronoun in this question is replacing **medicina**, which is singular and feminine. Singular eliminates C, and feminine gets rid of A. **Le** is an indirect object pronoun, and in this case no preposition is used.

27. After two years of research, the doctor finally ...
    a cure for the disease.

    (A) discovered
    (B) directed
    (C) opened
    (D) looked for

This is a very difficult question with a nasty second choice. If you understood *cure* you could have eliminated B and C because *directing* and *opening* a *cure* don't make sense. *Looked for* is tricky, but *after two years of research* makes A the best answer.

28. We've never danced the samba, but we sure
    _____ how to dance the lambada!

    (A) know (nosotros)
    (B) know (yo)
    (C) know (ellos)
    (D) know (nosotros)

Knowing how to do a type of dance falls under the category of facts (as opposed to people), so **saber** is the correct verb. Since the subject of the sentence is **nosotros**, **saben** is incorrect.

29. They say that José Martí, the famous Cuban
    author, began writing ... when he was only six
    years old.

    (A) pencils
    (B) alphabets
    (C) languages
    (D) poems

What does an author write? Well, lots of things, but out of these choices only D is reasonable.

Answers and Explanations: Part B

Emma dejó caer el papel. Su primera <u>impresión</u> fue de malestar en el vientre y en las rodillas; luego de ciega culpa, de irrealidad, de frío, de <u>temor</u>; luego, quiso ya <u>estar</u> en el día siguiente. Acto continuo comprendió que esa voluntad era inútil porque <u>la</u> muerte de su padre era lo único que <u>había sucedido</u> en el mundo, y <u>seguiría</u> sucediendo sin fin. Recogió el papel y se fue a su cuarto. Furtivamente lo <u>guardó</u> en un cajón, como si de algún modo ya <u>conociera</u> los hechos ulteriores.

Emma dropped the piece of paper. Her first impression was of a weak feeling in her stomach and in her knees; then of blind guilt, of unreality, of coldness, of fear; then she wished that it were already the next day. Immediately afterwards she realized that that wish was futile because the death of her father was the only thing that had happened in the world, and it would go on happening endlessly. She picked up the paper and went to her room. Furtively, she hid it in a drawer, as if somehow she already knew the subsequent facts.

30. (A)   time
    (B)   sight
    (C)   place
    (D)   impression

In this sentence, Emma's initial reaction to a letter is being described. The word that makes sense in the blank has to be something along the lines of "reaction." Of the choices offered, only **impresión** is even remotely similar to "reaction."

31. (A)   youth
    (B)   fear
    (C)   joy
    (D)   hunger

At this point in the paragraph, you know from the rest of Emma's reactions that she's not feeling so well, and the blank should be filled with a word that's consistent with her bad reactions. The only really negative choice is **temor**. If you weren't sure whether she was feeling good or bad, you should have skipped this and read on—later we find out that her father has died, which tells you for sure how she's feeling.

32. (A)   be
    (B)   be
    (C)   will be
    (D)   go

So we know Emma isn't happy. It makes sense that she'd want <u>to be</u> in the next day. That eliminates C and D, but does this situation call for **estar** or **ser**? Being in the next day is a temporary state, so **estar** is correct. Another approach to this question is to use the preposition that follows the blank (**en**). **Ir en** means to go by (as in **ir en avión** . . .), which makes no sense at all in this blank. Also, **quíso** (wanted to) implies the past, and so that tells you that **estaré** is wrong because it's the future tense.

33. (A)   the (lo)
     (B)   the (el)
     (C)   the (la)
     (D)   the·(las)

Muerte is a singular feminine noun, so the proper article is **la**.

34. (A)   entered
     (B)   grew
     (C)   had finished
     (D)   had happened

It doesn't make sense that the death of her father would enter or grow (cancel A and B). **Había terminado** is possible, but if you read on you find out that in fact Emma feels that it will go on affecting her. So the best answer is D.

35. **(A)   would continue**
     (B)   would stop
     (C)   would change
     (D)   would feel

This is sort of a continuation of the last question. The expression **sin fin** (without end) is a big clue here, because it tells you that Emma's going to be unhappy for a long time. The fact that her grief is ongoing without end really only leaves one possible answer, and that's **seguiría**.

36. (A)   took out
     (B)   put away
     (C)   found
     (D)   took off

In this sentence, Emma does something with her letter. Since we know she already has it and has read it, A and C wouldn't make sense. **Quitó** is just strange, so that leaves us with B.

37. (A)   knows
     (B)   doubted
     (C)   knew
     (D)   began

The saving grace on this question is the **si** that comes just before the blank, which tells you to use the conditional. Luckily only one choice is in the conditional, because this would be a very tough question to do based on meaning alone.

Después <u>de</u> haber mandado dos expediciones a explorar la costa de México, el gobernador de Cuba <u>organizó</u> otra expedición bajo el mando de Hernán Cortés en 1519. En las tres expediciones <u>tomó</u> parte un soldado que se <u>llamaba</u> Bernal Díaz del Castillo. <u>Este</u> soldado, cuando ya era casi viejo y <u>vivía</u> retirado en Guatemala, <u>escribió</u> sus recuerdos de las guerras mexicanas, que forman la mejor narración <u>sobre</u> la conquista de México y que se titula "Historia verdadera de la conquista de la nueva España."
La expedición de Cortés constaba de once navíos que <u>llevaban</u> poco más de seiscientos hombres y dieciséis <u>caballos</u>. Cuando estaba listo Cortés <u>para</u> salir, el gobernador trató de quitarle el mando, pero él decidió hacerse a la mar.

After having led two expeditions to explore the coast of Mexico, the governor of Cuba organized another expedition under the command of Hernán Cortés in 1519. In the three expeditions a soldier whose name was Bernal Díaz (of) Castillo took part. This soldier, when he was already old and retired in Guatemala, wrote his memoirs of the Mexican wars, which constitute the best narrative about the conquest of Mexico and are titled "True History of the Conquest of New Spain."

Cortés's expedition consisted of eleven ships that carried little more than six hundred men and sixteen horses. When Cortés was ready to leave, the governor tried to take command from him, but he decided to take off.

38. (A) that
    (B) of
    (C) to
    (D) for

The preposition that follows **después** to mean "after" is **de**. It's on your list of prepositions.

39. (A) put an end to
    (B) rehearsed
    (C) asked
    (D) organized

The only answers that make any kind of sense in the blank are A and D. How do we know whether the governor organized or put an end to the next expedition? We know a third one happened because in the very next sentence it talks about three expeditions. By skipping a question and reading on you can sometimes find a clue that helps answer an earlier question.

40. (A)   made
    (B)   gave
    (C)   left
    (D)   took

Although a couple of the answers are a bit awkward in the blank (namely A and C), it really helps on this question if you know the expression **tomar parte**, meaning to take part. If you didn't know this expression, you should've canceled A and C and guessed.

41. (A)   was named
    (B)   is named
    (C)   was named
    (D)   had been named

Here, what you want to say is "was named." We know it's going to be some kind of past tense, but which past tense is appropriate? Well, a person's name goes on for a period of time, so it's not the regular past. In this case the person that's referred to is deceased, so the action can't be continuing into the present. That leaves the imperfect.

42. **(A)   This (masc.)**
    (B)   That (fem.)
    (C)   A (masc.)
    (D)   What (neut.)

Soldado is masculine, so B is immediately out. The sentence goes on to discuss the soldier in question, so what you want to say is "this soldier."

43. (A)   stopped
    (B)   thought
    (C)   heard
    (D)   lived

Look at the adjective that follows the blank (**retirado**). Even if you've never seen this word before, you can tell what it means because it's just like the English equivalent. Does a person stop retired, *think* retired, or *hear* retired? None of those makes sense, so that leaves only D.

44. **(A)   wrote**
    (B)   ran
    (C)   lost
    (D)   asked for

The blank in this case precedes **recuerdos**, which can mean memories. However, in this case it means memoirs, which is a hint that something having to do with writing (like **escribió**) would be the correct answer. If you missed **recuerdos**, the word **título** is mentioned later on, followed by a title with quotes. Look around for clues, don't just stick to the immediate area where the blank is.

45. (A)   on top of
    (B)   next to
    (C)   on; about
    (D)   instead of

The meaning you want for this blank is roughly "about," because you're providing a preposition that describes the relationship between the memoirs and their subject (memoirs are <u>about</u> a subject). **Encima de** means "on," like "on top of" or "above," not "about," **En vez de** and **junto a** don't mean anything close to "about."

46. (A)   took
    (B)   took
    (C)   took
    (D)   take

The verb (**llevar**) in this blank refers back to the plural subject **navios**, so you know the answer must be plural, which leave B, C, and D. If you back up just a bit earlier in the sentence, you notice that we're in the imperfect tense (**constaba** tells you). Even if you only knew it was some type of past tense you could eliminate D (**llevan** is present tense) and guess.

47. (A)   cars
    (B)   airplanes
    (C)   horses
    (D)   gloves

The big hint on this question is that the passage deals with events that happened in the late sixteenth century, before the invention of the airplane and the automobile. *Gloves* <u>could</u> work, but *horses* (a means of transportation) is a much more likely answer.

48. (A)   for
    (B)   to
    (C)   in
    (D)   of

This question asks for the preposition that precedes **salir**. Although C and D make no sense, that still leaves you with the decision between **para** and **por**. In this case the meaning you want is "to," so **para** is correct.

Pero hoy, esta mañana fría, en que tenemos más prisa que nunca, la niña y yo <u>pasamos</u> de largo delante de la fila tentadora de autos parados. Por <u>primera</u> vez en la vida vamos al colegio... Al colegio, le digo, no <u>se puede</u> ir en taxi. Hay que correr un poco por las calles, hay que tomar el metro, hay que <u>caminar</u> luego, en un sitio determinado, a un autobús... Es que yo he escogido un colegio muy <u>lejano</u> para mi niña, ésa es la verdad; un colegio que <u>me gusta</u> mucho, pero está muy lejos... Sin embargo, yo no estoy impaciente hoy, ni <u>cansada</u>, y la niña lo sabe. Es ella ahora la que inicia una caricia tímida con su manita <u>dentro de</u> la mía; y por primera vez me doy cuenta de que su mano de cuatro años es <u>igual a</u> mi mano grande: tan decidida, tan poco suave, tan nerviosa como la mía.

But today, on this cold morning, on which we're in a bigger hurry than ever, the girl and I pass by the tempting line of waiting cars. For the first time in our lives we're going to school... To school, I tell her, you cannot go by taxi. You have to run through the streets a bit, take the subway, then later walk to the appropriate place to catch the bus... It's that I've chosen a school that's very far for my daughter, that is the truth of the matter; a school that I like very much, but it is very far away. Nonetheless, I'm not impatient today, nor tired, and the girl knows it. It is now she who initiates a timid caress with her little hand inside mine; and for the first time I realize that her four-year-old hand is the same as my adult one: just as resolute, rough, and nervous as mine.

49. **(A)** **we passed**
    (B)   we went in
    (C)   we gave
    (D)   we paid

The preposition **delante de** (in front of) that comes shortly after the blank is the main clue on this question. The only verb that makes sense before this expression is A.

50. (A)   none
    (B)   **first**
    (C)   always
    (D)   habit

The word **vez** (time, occasion) immediately follows the blank, and the only choice that forms an expression in conjunction with **vez** is B.

51. (A) tricks herself
    (B) know
    (C) can
    (D) to have surplus

The sentence is about getting to school by taxi. Earlier in the passage it says that they passed by a row of taxis. But that only gets rid of A and D because we don't know why they passed by the taxis. If you think about B carefully though, it doesn't make sense. <u>They</u> wouldn't have to know how to get to school in a taxi, the <u>taxi driver</u> would.

52. (A) sleep
    (B) touch
    (C) play
    (D) walk

You wouldn't *sleep, touch,* or *play* in order to get to a bus stop. Walking, on the other hand, seems likely.

53. (A) closed
    (B) far away
    (C) dark
    (D) difficult

This blank describes the type of school that the mother chose for her daughter. Common sense eliminates A and C. If you're stuck at this point, you just need to look forward a bit to find the clue that singles out B as the best answer: **"esta muy lejos."**

54. **(A) I like**
    (B) I hate
    (C) I don't know
    (D) we doubt

The blank is followed by the expression **pero está muy lejos.** The **pero** tells you that a positive quality about the school came immediately before the expression (the word "but" indicates a contrast, as in "strict <u>but</u> fair"). This gets rid of B and D, and C makes no sense because the mother in the passage chose this school for her daughter, whom she seems to love very much. Would she send her daughter to a school she didn't know?! Probably not.

55. (A)   old
    (B)   tall
    (C)   tired
    (D)   fresh

The verb **estar** is used in this sentence, and that eliminates **vieja** because **vieja** would be used with **ser** (ella **es** vieja). The same is true for **alta** (ella **es** alta). **Fresca** is a word you might use for fruit or vegetables in Spanish, but it's not used to describe a person's condition (even though in English we might say "My student was acting fresh").

56. **(A)   inside of**
    (B)   outside of
    (C)   close to
    (D)   without

Her the daughter is making an effectionate gesture (**caricia**) toward her mom by putting her hand somewher in relation to her mom's hand. Choices B and D suggest just the opposite, as if she were making a negative gesture. Anser C is O.K., but really doesn't make a lot of sense if you really think about it: you wouldn't put your hand *close to* someone else's to show affection, you'd put your hand *in* someone else's.

57. (A)   different from
    (B)   equal to, the same as
    (C)   close to
    (D)   on top of

The giveaway for this question follows the blank: **tan**. **Tan** by itself means "so," but the expression **tan...como** means "equal to."

Answers and Explanations: Part C

While passing by a farm, a dog bit my friend. We went in to see the farmer and asked if the dog were his. The farmer, in order to avoid trouble, said it was not his.

—Then—said my friend—lend me a scythe so I can cut his head off, then I should take it to the Institute so they can analyze it.

At that moment the farmer's daughter appeared and asked her father not to let us cut off the dog's head.

—If the dog is yours—said my friend—show the certificate of rabies vaccination.

The man went into the farmhouse, and took a long time to come back out. Meanwhile, the dog came closer and my friend said:

—I don't like the way this animal looks.

Essentially, he foamed at the mouth and his eyes looked like they burned in their sockets. He also moved in an odd way.

—A few days ago—said the girl—he was run over by a bicycle.

The farmer told us that he couldn't find the certificate of vaccination.

—I probably lost it.

—The life of a man could be at stake—I interjected—Tell us, in all honesty, whether the dog is vaccinated or not.

The man bowed his head and murmured:
—He's healthy.

58. What happened to the men when they passed the farm?

(A) a dog bit one of them
(B) a farmer asked them for directions
(C) it started to rain
(D) they lost their dog

The answer to this question is in the first sentence of the passage. Normally the progression of the questions follows the progression of the passage. The earlier a question is, the earlier in the passage you'll find its answer, etc.

59. Why did the farmer say the dog wasn't his?

(A) he didn't know whose the dog was
(B) he didn't know the men who came to the door
(C) he didn't want to take blame for what the dog had done
(D) he didn't like dogs

In the passage (third line) it says that the farmer wanted to **evitarse complicaciones** (avoid trouble). The answer closest to that in meaning is C. Some of the other answers are reasonable, but they aren't in the passage.

60. What did the farmer's daughter request of him?

(A) that he give her money for candy
(B) that he take the dog to the doctor
(C) that he feed the dog
(D) that he not let the men hurt the dog

The guide word for this question is **hija.** The first place where **hija** appears (and the source of the answer) is toward the beginning.

61. What did the men ask the farmer for?

(A) a glass of water
(B) the certificate of rabies vaccination
(C) a telephone to call the police with
(D) proof that he was really a farmer

62. How does the farmer's dog seem?

(A) healthy and in good humor
(B) sick, as if rabid
(C) youthful and full of energy
(D) serious and thoughtful

Most of the passage is concerned with vaccinations (**vacunaciones**) and whether or not to cut the dog's head off and have it inspected. You probably wouldn't do this to a happy, healthy dog (unless you're some kind of sick weirdo) so you can eliminate A and C immediately. You probably wouldn't decapitate a dog for being "**serio y pensativo**" either, so D is out. That leaves you with B. Pretty simple.

63. What reason did the girl give for the way the dog behaved?

(A) it had an accident with a bicycle
(B) it doesn't like people
(C) it's a very vicious dog
(D) it was very hungry

Once again, this question deals with the daughter, who is re-ferred to as **la joven** as well as **hija** and **niña** in different parts of the passage.

64. Finally, what does the farmer tell the men?

(A) that they should go to a hospital
(B) that they should adopt a dog
(C) that they should leave the farm right now
(D) that the dog has no disease

En fin is a pretty strong hint that the answer's toward the end. The correct choice is D.

> In our office, the same budget has been in operation since the nineteen twenties, that is, since a time when most of us were struggling with geometry and fractions. Our Chief, however, remembered the great event, and sometimes, when there wasn't so much work, he would sit down familiarly on one of our desks, and there, with his legs dangling, and immaculate white socks showing below his trousers, he would tell us, with all his old feeling and with his usual five hundred and ninety-eight words, of that distant and splendid day when his Chief—he was a Head Clerk then—patted him on the shoulder and said "My boy, we're having a new budget," with the broad and satisfied smile of a man who has already worked out how many new shirts he will be able to buy with the increase.

65. For about how much time have they had the same budget?

(A) for many decades
(B) for many centuries
(C) for a few weeks
(D) since yesterday

There are a few answers (namely B, C, and D) that are pretty silly in the context of the story, but this is more apparent as you read further into the passage. If you didn't get **novecientos veintitantos**, then you should have read on. There are lots of clues later on that give you the time frame of the budget.

66. The Chief told his story when

(A) he was sad
(B) he had drunk too much beer
(C) there was less work than usual
(D) they had a party

Disminuía means decreased or diminished. **Jefe** is one guide word on this question, and **cuento** is sort of another, although **acontecimiento** is the actual word in the passage (**cuento** looks similar).

67. The story of the new budget that the Chief told

   (A) had white socks
   (B) was always different
   (C) was interesting
   (D) was always the same

Palabras de costumbre (usual words) is the key to this one.

68. What was the chief's reaction when his Chief told
   him about the new budget?

   (A) he left the company
   (B) he became very happy
   (C) he gave his chief a hug
   (D) he bought new shirts

Answer D is a pretty nasty trap, but if you read carefully you could have avoided it.

> For archaeologists and historians, the Mayan civilization is, without a doubt, the one that reached the highest level of development of all the civilizations that existed before the arrival of Columbus. Although there are still many secrets that have not been deciphered with regard to the Mayas, it appears that this civilization began many centuries before the birth of Christ. Nonetheless, it's known that the Mayas abandoned their large ceremonial centers in the tenth century of our era.
>
> The first temples they built were pyramid shaped with four faces and a huge outside stairway. On top of the pyramid there is an edifice that is normally one story, and in some cases two, and in them we can see clay reliefs and statues made of wood and limestone. The figures are always in profile and in them you can see the decorations and jewels they used. In the classification that has been made of the epochs of this civilization, the first, which developed in Guatemala and Honduras, is called the pre-classic era and, according to archaeologists, lasted until the end of our third century.

69. What do the archaeologists and historians think
   of the Mayan civilization?

   (A) that it was a very advanced civilization
   (B) that the Mayans wrote wonderful books
   (C) that they knew Columbus
   (D) that they had many secrets

Arqueólogos and **historiadores** are the guide words here.

70.   When did the Mayan civilization begin?

(A) in the tenth century of our era
(B) immediately before Columbus's arrival
(C) many centuries before Christ's birth
(D) many centuries after Christ's birth

It's technically not a guide word, but **cuando** tells you that you want to look for a date or year.

71.   What did the first Mayan temples look like?

(A) they were very short buildings
(B) they were made of wood and limestone
(C) they were pyramids with four faces
(D) they were ordinary houses, like the ones we have today

Templos is your guide for this question.

72.   What can be said about the Mayan sculptures?

(A) they had large staircases
(B) they give information about the jewels and decorations that they used
(C) it costs a lot to buy them
(D) they can be found in famous museums

Esculturas tells you where to look, but you've still got to read with care.

73.   Where did the development of the pre-classic era begin?

(A) in Nicaragua
(B) in Mexico
(C) in the pre-classic era
(D) in Honduras and Guatemala

Preclásica only appears at the end of the passage, which is where the answer lies.

74.   The passage deals with

(A) Mayan civilization and architecture
(B) Christ's influence on Mayan civilization
(C) the difference between our civilizatioin and Mayan civilization
(D) the ornaments and jewels used by the Mayans

This one's a little tricky. The passge does mention Christ (**Cristo**), whose name appears in B, and ornaments and jewels (**adornos y joyas**), which appear in answer choice D, but it also deals with other stuff. B and D are too specific. Omit them. The passage doesn't specifically compare Mayan culture to any other culture, including ours, so C is out. That leaves A, a nice, general, correct answer.

> In a few years it will be five centuries since the meeting of Europe and America. It was shortly after midnight between the 11th and 12th of October in 1492, when Rodrigo de Triana, a crew member of the ship "La Niña," which had gone ahead of "The Santa María," where Columbus was, let out the shout of "Land, land." The place was very close to Florida, a small island named Guanahani which Columbus gave the name San Salvador and which belongs to the archipelago of the Lucayas or Bahamas.
>
> What Columbus found and described in his letters to the Catholic king and queen was much poverty and people who went naked, the way their mothers bore them, all of them young, with beautiful bodies, thick heads of hair like a horse's which fell over their eyebrows and which others wore long in back.
>
> A few days later, he discovered the coast of Cuba, which he named Juana, after the daughter of the king and queen. At that point, Martin Alonzo Pinzon, who captained "The Pinta," pulled away from the expedition, which Columbus considered an act of desertion, although he pretended not to notice in order to maintain the unity of the expedition. After a few days he reached Haiti, which he named The Spaniard, but due to the many sandbanks and reefs that there were, "The Santa María" ran aground.

75. Who was the first to see land in the expedition?

    (A) a sailor named Rodrigo de Triana
    (B) Columbus
    (C) The Niña
    (D) Guanahani, Columbus's best friend

You can knock off C without looking back at the passage. Once you look back, the answer is in that sentence. **Tierra** is what you're looking for.

76. What were the people who Columbus found like?

    (A) very poor, but also beautiful
    (B) violent and agressive
    (C) smarter than the sailors
    (D) very scared and confused

This question doesn't really have guide words, but luckily there is an entire paragraph about this topic so it shouldn't have been too tough to locate the source of the question.

77. What did Columbus discover a few days after he discovered San Salvador?

   (A) the archipelago of the Bahamas
   (B) the island that is today known as Cuba
   (C) Haiti
   (D) thick hair

This ia a tricky question, because it's easy to think that **San Salvador** is the guide, when actually **pocos días después** is your clue on this one. If you have trouble locating the source of a question, just skip it and come back to it later.

78. What was Columbus's reaction when Martín Alonzo Pinzón separated from the expedition?

   (A) he became furious
   (B) he started to cry
   (C) he gave the impression that he didn't know what had happened
   (D) he sent another ship after him

The name is the guide on this one, and it only appears once.

79. How did the Santa María end up?

   (A) it returned to Spain
   (B) it was lost and never found
   (C) it sank
   (D) it ran aground as a result of reefs and shallows

The name of the ship is the big clue here. The location of the question tells you to look towards the end of the passage.

If it weren't for the demanding taste of the coffee drinkers of Saudi Arabia, the Guatemalan town of Cobán, on the other side of the world, would be in big trouble.

Cobán, capital of the mountainous region of Alta Verapaz in Guatemala, is the source of the majority of cardamom that the Arab world consumes: a sweet spice, pungent and extremely aromatic that is used in the cooking of India. As a matter of fact, coffee with cardamom known in the Arab world as *kahwe hal,* is considered a symbol of hospitality in all the Near East.

In Cobán, famous for its 16th-century Catholic church and the Mayan ruins that are found on its borders, practically no one speaks Arabic and none of its 125,000 inhabitants puts cardamom in his coffee. Nevertheless, they all know perfectly well the connection that exists between the spice and the Arab world. "Cardamom is the base of our economy, and Guatemala is its principal exporter in the world."

80. In which country in particular do they drink coffee with cardamom?

(A) in Guatemala
(B) in Saudi Arabia
(C) in Alta Verapaz
(D) in the Near East

A couple of answers (the ones that aren't countries) can be eliminated right away.

81. What is cardamom?

(A) a rare type of coffee
(B) a spice
(C) an Indian style of cooking
(D) a type of tree

Even if you'd never seen the word **especia**, POE works really well on this question.

82. How does cardamom taste?

(A) sharp, but also sweet
(B) a bit bitter
(C) it hardly has any flavor
(D) it tastes like Colombian coffee

The answer to this one is in the paragraph that describes the spice.

83. For what is the city of Cobán known?

(A) for cardamom
(B) for the best coffee in North America
**(C) for its ruins, and for its 16th century
    church**
(D) for the Indian food

Choice A is an easy trap to fall for if you're lazy on this one and don't look back. For those who weren't lazy, the answer is right at the top of the final paragraph. Look back to the passage on the specific questions.

84. What is the connection between the Arab world
     and Guatemala?

(A) in Guatemala everyone speaks Arabic
(B) in both places they love coffee with carda-
    mom
**(C) Guatemala exports much of the spice to
    the Arab world**
(D) there really is no connection between the
    two places

Although the answer to this one is in the last paragraph (**conexión** is your guide), the relationship is mentioned earlier in the passage as well.

85. What would be a good title for the passage?

(A) "Cobán: the city in the mountains"
(B) "The economy of Guatemala"
(C) "The coffees of the world"
**(D) "Cardamom: what joins Guatemala with
    the Arab world"**

Remember, the answer to a question like this must include the ideas of the whole passage. B is only a partially correct answer (it's not wrong, but it doesn't tell the whole story).

NOTES

NOTES

NOTES

NOTES

NOTES

NOTES

NOTES

NOTES

NOTES

NOTES

NOTES

NOTES

ABOUT THE AUTHOR

George Roberto Pace was born in Miami in 1966. The native Spanish speaker moved to New York City at the age of two months, where he grew up and attended Hunter College High School. He received his B.A. from Oberlin College in 1988, and he currently resides in Chicago where he is Director of the Princeton Review of the Great Plains.

The Princeton Review
Diagnostic Test Form ○ Side 1

1.

YOUR NAME: _____
(Print)   Last   First   M.I.

SIGNATURE: _____   DATE: ___ / ___ / ___

HOME ADDRESS: _____
(Print)   Number and Street

_____
City   State   Zip Code

PHONE NO.: _____
(Print)

IMPORTANT: Please fill in these boxes exactly as shown on the back cover of your test book.

2. TEST FORM

3. TEST CODE

4. REGISTRATION NUMBER

5. YOUR NAME

First 4 letters of last name				FIRST INIT	MID INIT

6. DATE OF BIRTH

MONTH	DAY	YEAR
JAN		
FEB		
MAR		
APR		
MAY		
JUN		
JUL		
AUG		
SEP		
OCT		
NOV		
DEC		

7. SEX
○ MALE
○ FEMALE

SCANTRON® FORM NO. F-592-KIN
© SCANTRON CORPORATION 1989   3289-C553-5 4 3 2 1
ALL RIGHTS RESERVED.

Begin with number 1 for each new section of the test. Leave blank any extra answer spaces.

SECTION 1

(Answer bubbles A B C D E for questions 1–100)

The Princeton Review
Diagnostic Test Form ○ Side 2

Completely darken bubbles with a No. 2 pencil. If you make a mistake, be sure to erase mark completely. Erase all stray marks.

Begin with number 1 for each new section of the test. Leave blank any extra answer spaces.

SECTION 2

SECTION 3

FOR TPR USE ONLY | V1 | V2 | V3 | V4 | M1 | M2 | M3 | M4 | M5 | M6 | M7 | M8